Making AI Sense-Like

Jorge Argibay

Published by Jorge Argibay, 2024.

While every precaution has been taken in the preparation of this book, the publisher assumes no responsibility for errors or omissions, or for damages resulting from the use of the information contained herein.

MAKING AI SENSE-LIKE

First edition. January 13, 2024.

Copyright © 2024 Jorge Argibay.

ISBN: 979-8224366453

Written by Jorge Argibay.

Table of Contents

Prologue

Does the AI have its own neurons?. Can store and redirect them towards a higher reasoning?. Can they embody and guide a mutual common sense between people and machine?. These are questions that demand an answer, equations that require a mathematical solution, posed in a universe of innovation and audacity.

The human brain houses billions of neurons, each of which produces thousands of connections. A byte consists of 8 bits, and the human brain can store more than a quadrillion bytes of data - a petabyte. We assume that they will be enough for an average and acceptable common sense.

The human brain routes and transports signals and signs throughout the body. Various signals control processes, and the brain reads each of them. Multiple messages are retained within the brain. Others are communicated through the spinal column and the huge territories of nerves in the body up to length limits.

What about AI, does it have sensory, short term and long term memory, can the brain of a machine send, collect and ultimately store diverse data and various information and direct it from the cortex, where the brain's nerve cells are stored, to the hippocampus to store the memory?.

Although computers and modern storage gadgets have proven to be an incredible modern marvel, the human brain is still credited as the world's most powerful thinking machine. At least to this day. But the behaviour of both sides has changed, and the hostile nature of the surroundings makes it necessary to be cautious.

The rapprochement between what is traditional and what AI offers is increasingly tense, there are dissenting voices that do not want to use these new tools, but the technology is evolving and, like other innovations of the past, it is making its way firmly and forcefully. Whether or not it is supported by neurons.

There is value in asking questions about how AI thinks, how it manages its inner workings. There is a need to understand how the creative blades of tools that are innovative but still produce their own hidden sense of a certain opacity turn. It is a need for knowledge of the unknown across a broad evolutionary spectrum.

The review of different reasoning options sets the creative tone of this paper, which will reflect the versatile and transformative aspects in the context of AI. On the other hand, it will reflect individual patterns of business approach, where AI feeds and conditions the new tasks of the different teams on a daily basis.

These approaches will be dealt with more extensively in the second part, giving our review a closeness where the AI is blurred between the tentacles of the most corpulent business.

The semantic relationships between words and concepts, the links between the linguistic and mathematical worlds, the assessments in the natural language processing environment, the cognitive skills on offer, the reasoning that leads to problem solving and the archetypal world of problem solving will come into play and demonstrate their skills and abilities.

Not forgetting the concepts of 'Common Sense Reasoning' and 'Analogical Reasoning', which are central to this bifurcation of basic emotions to create AI systems that perform tasks that require human-like thinking and problem-solving skills. They make their contribution in parallel, completely good-natured and without fuss.

These contributions are fundamental to the development of a narrative that will take the reader from an external environment seeking to delve into the interior of its own unknown, to the unknown centre of AI. There will be clarifying and varied examples in its understanding, for there are many issues to be addressed.

It will also try to circulate the thought of distrust as to whether the information obtained through IA can be considered reliable, and at the same time, the guidelines to confront the permanent innovative changes of an environment that does not look backwards, only towards the future.

And here I have two buts. But, the amount of information we find in any search today is massive, so we come to the point of difficulty, which is to make the appropriate selection and, more importantly, to avoid false information in favour of true information. We need clarity of thought, knowing what we are looking for is not enough, we need to be critical and choose the option or options of importance or relevance.

But software changes all the time. Managing programmes sometimes requires no more than training, even at a business level, but software, new programmes emerge and appear with the ease of raindrops in the middle of winter. Anyone can go to a specialised website and see the number of programmes that are created every day, or more precisely, the number of updates.

This question makes many users nervous, because although it can be motivating to learn new software, it is also stressful for many users to know that they are preparing for this programme, but that there will be an update soon. This creates frustration for many people who wonder why the learning process cannot give them a minimum of continuity time.

Another point is that of people who feel that there is no benefit to them in their lives from using AI technology, and who choose not to use it. Some people talk about technological illiterates, what does that mean?. They mean someone who does not know how to turn on a PC. They mean those who cannot use basic software tools such as word processors?. You mean those who don't know how to program?.

In most cases, a person's interest is more than enough to achieve the most basic steps. If the decision is to know how to use technology at a user level, this can be achieved in any public library that offers a basic course or two. It is another thing to know how to program or to achieve 'high scale' goals, but no one will be left behind if they want to.

In the wider context of usability, it can be said that any PC, laptop, tablet, mobile phone or other device is really easy to use, at least in its most basic functions. The question would be to identify the areas of improvement for each of these 'illiterates' and offer them guarantees of individual and autonomous usability.

We can all access a computer, open basic functions and use them with a few simple instructions or even by following a manual. Typing into the search engine is as easy as it gets, so finding accessible information is effortless. The only thing missing is the selection, getting the right one, not the wrong one.

Even under these constraints, the goal of AI should be to improve the people condition, not to exacerbate existing inequalities or to address potential structural and environmental problems in our societies.

Developers of AI services and products are likely to be at the heart of this challenge: they are the ones who directly prevent errors and biases in input data or future applications. They represent a priori knowledge that lead to or prevent misuse (conscious or unconscious).

These will not be the only parameters of the AI's reasoning ability and variables addressed, we will dive into a vast lake of AI systems, predictive environment or cultural approach.

Without forgetting aspects such as cultural content recommendations, cultural intelligence (CQ), cross-cultural communication enhancement, contrasting their contributions in this AI context, how they facilitate alternative approaches and phases of approach, how they guide greater effectiveness and interactions in the cross-cultural atmosphere.

The cross-cultural environment is not always an easy path, but on the contrary is full of hurdles that make it difficult to move forward correctly. AI systems will create their own contributions or extend and improve existing ones, with a clear and manifest vision of intuitive progress.

It will always be in this perspective that the virtual, let's say virtual reality (VR) or augmented reality (AR) transport users to historical periods or cultural events, by immersing oneself in parallel zones that will help one's own understanding of a reality that needs to be falsified for its pitiful evolution.

In the AI-supported business world (as we will see in the second part), strategy becomes the foundation for action and daily investment between employees, third-party needs, managers and the future evolution of the company (more on strategy).

In this business world, AI underpins and accelerates or, in other words, directly and even aggressively manages the company's productivity. AI systems extend their tentacles once again and are creating a universe of tasks, data collection and processing activities, which will always be enlisted with a mix of very active and complex vision.

This complexity of tasks will be simplified for the sake of greater acceptability of employees and greater stability of knowledge and management of managers. There will be no pause, there will be no room for rest, on the contrary, actions will evolve in a circular environment of excess and business acceptance.

Of course we will need to adopt strategies, they will help us to discern the best way to reach the client, they will channel the options of success of our beginnings, they will be or rather it will be (the chosen one) who will mark our constant possibilities of improvement and satisfaction, in an AI environment that is approaching of the most competitive.

Sometimes the strategist includes people who possess the ability to rise to an occasion and deliver value that is least expected of them. It is difficult to tipify the exact nature of AI strategy. For example, organizational functions such as sales, marketing or engineering have clearly defined tasks and competencies. The qualities that AI strategist need to possess are varuied and diverse.

Sometimes it will be the strategy of AI-Integrated Digital Transformation, sometimes it will be AI-Driven Mergers and Acquisitions (M&A) or whichever variant is needed in this AI context. Whatever the type of strategy, it will enhance and reinforce important aspects, such as, driving innovation, boosting efficiency or fostering growth of the company.

AI is driving process automation and optimization across various business functions. By automating repetitive and manual tasks, AI-powered systems can significantly improve operational efficiency and productivity. This integration also makes automation more resilient and adaptable to changes, which is particularly important in dynamic business environments.

A traves de la AI-enhanced market segmentation strategy, tendremos a mano una serie de funcionalidades, designed to enhance customer segmentation efforts, including, automated segmentation, behavioral analysis, predictive modeling and dynamic audience segmentation.

Other types of strategy will complete the review, thus AI-powered market expansion, AI-enhanced product diversification, AI-Driven cost leadership, AI-infused differentiation, AI-infused sustainability and corporate responsibility.

The perspectives in the role of AI finance are converted into knowledge, record their assumptions well in advance and get these resolved by sharing these with team members, we refer (among others) to risk management and fraud detection, customer service and personalization and regulatory compliance.

It makes sense for companies to cut down on the uncertainty when they want to venture into a new area. Venturing into areas in which organizations have lesser knowledge and that have contexts that are different from the organizations existing business context is not a good idea. When organizations minimize the number of uncertainties they reduce the risk. A good way to venture into a new area is to break a long-term project into smaller pieces that can be managed well.

As productivity support we can choose the most appropriate software, we will mention some that have been personally managed both individually and in groups. Their alternatives are valid, straightforward and of course productive. Workday, Service now or Slack are are tools worth trusting, they always manage and guide in a positive direction, whatever the team in which we are involved. This will be the last rung on the ladder of ascent to complete our narrative.

FIRST PART

1. The AI's Reasoning Ability.

AI is important for its potential to change how we live, work and play. It has been effectively used in business to automate tasks done by people, including customer service work, lead generation, fraud detection and quality control.

In a number of areas, AI can perform tasks much better than people. Particularly when it comes to repetitive, detail-oriented tasks, such as analyzing large numbers of legal documents to ensure relevant fields are filled in properly, AI tools often complete jobs quickly and with relatively few errors.

Because of the massive data sets it can process, also give enterprises insights into their operations they might not have been aware of. The rapidly expanding population of generative AI tools will be important in fields ranging from education and marketing to product design.

AI holds immense significance due to its transformative potential in shaping our lifestyles, professions, and leisure activities. Its integration into businesses has revolutionized operations by automating human tasks, encompassing areas like customer service, lead generation, fraud detection, and quality control.

AI excels, especially in tasks demanding precision and repetition, such as meticulously analyzing vast legal documents to ensure accurate data input. These tools complete assignments swiftly and with minimal errors. Moreover, AI's ability to process massive datasets provides valuable insights into operations, previously unknown to enterprises.

The expanding realm of generative AI tools plays a pivotal role across diverse fields like education, marketing, and product design, signifying its indispensability in the future landscape. Advances in AI techniques have not only helped fuel an explosion in efficiency, but opened the door to entirely new business opportunities for some larger enterprises.

Prior to the current wave of AI, it would have been hard to imagine using computer software to connect riders to taxis, but Uber has become a Fortune 500 company by doing just that. AI has become central to many of today's largest and most successful companies, including Alphabet, Apple, Microsoft and Meta, where AI technologies are used to improve operations and outpace competitors.

At Alphabet subsidiary Google, for example, AI is central to its search engine, Waymo's self-driving cars and Google Brain, which invented the transformer neural network architecture that underpins the recent breakthroughs in natural language processing.

• • • •

How does the AI perform?.

• • • •

AI is relevant because of its potential to change the way we experience lifestyles, work and leisure. It has been efficiently implemented in businesses to automate tasks performed by people, such as customer service work, lead generation, fraud detection and quality control. In several areas, AI can perform tasks much better than people.

This is particularly true when it comes to repetitive and detail-oriented tasks, such as parsing large quantities of legal documents to ensure that the relevant fields are filled in appropriately.

AI tools often complete jobs quickly and with relatively few errors. Because of the huge data sets it can process, AI can also give businesses intelligence about their operations that they might not be aware of. The population of generative AI tools will be sizable in fields ranging from education and marketing to product design.

As the hype around AI has quickened, vendors have been quick to tout how their products and services use it. Often, what they call AI is simply a component of the technology, such as machine learning. AI requires a foundation of specialized hardware and software for writing and training machine learning algorithms. No single programming language is synonymous with AI, but Python, R, Java, C++ and Julia have features popular with AI developers.

In general, AI systems work by ingesting large amounts of labeled training data, analyzing the data for correlations and patterns, and using these patterns to make predictions about future states.

In this way, a chatbot that is fed examples of text can learn to generate lifelike exchanges with people, or an image recognition tool can learn to identify and describe objects in images by reviewing millions of examples. New, rapidly improving generative AI techniques can create realistic text, images, music and other media (veremos ejemplos mas adelante).

AI is categorized into three types, beginning with the task-specific intelligent systems in wide use today and progressing to theory of mind.

Reactive machines.

These systems lack memory and are designed for specific tasks. An illustrative example provided is Deep Blue, the IBM chess program that gained fame in the 1990s by defeating world champion Garry Kasparov. Deep Blue's capabilities include identifying chessboard pieces and making predictions. However, a crucial limitation is highlighted: these systems lack the ability to utilize past experiences to influence future decisions due to their absence of memory.

Another example is the Roomba robotic vacuum cleaner developed by iRobot. Roomba is designed for a specific task: cleaning floors. It uses sensors to detect obstacles and navigate around them while cleaning the floors in a systematic pattern. However, Roomba does not have memory or the ability to learn from past cleaning experiences.

Each cleaning session is independent, and it does not improve its cleaning performance based on previous encounters. Therefore, Roomba operates as a Reactive machine, solely focused on the task it is designed for without the ability to adapt or learn over time.

• • • •

Limited memory.

These AI systems possess the ability to retain and utilize past experiences for making future decisions. An illustrative example mentioned is the decision-making functions in self-driving cars, which are designed with limited memory capabilities. This enables the self-driving cars to learn from previous situations and use that knowledge to make informed decisions in real-time scenarios.

Another example will be found in recommendation algorithms used by online streaming platforms like Netflix. These algorithms remember users' past viewing history, preferences, and ratings to suggest movies and TV shows that align with their interests. By utilizing limited memory, these recommendation systems enhance user experience by providing tailored content suggestions based on their previous interactions with the platform.

Theory of mind.

Theory of mind is a psychology term. When applied to AI, it means the system would have the social intelligence to understand emotions. This type of AI will be able to infer human intentions and predict behavior, a necessary skill for AI systems to become integral members of human teams.

In the context of psychology, Theory of Mind refers to the ability to understand and interpret the thoughts, emotions, and intentions of others. When applied to AI, this term indicates a level of social intelligence where AI systems comprehend human emotions, infer intentions, and predict behavior.

This advanced capability is crucial for AI systems to seamlessly integrate into human teams, enabling them to understand the nuances of human interaction and collaborate effectively in various social and professional contexts.

An example of Type 3 AI, or Theory of Mind AI, would be seen in virtual assistants like Amazon's Alexa, Apple's Siri, and Google

Assistant. These AI systems are designed not only to recognize and process voice commands but also to understand the context and intent behind the user's words.

For instance, they distinguish between a casual inquiry and a specific command, interpreting the user's tone and intention through voice modulation and language nuances.

By comprehending the user's emotions and intentions, these virtual assistants provide more personalized and contextually relevant responses, showcasing a rudimentary form of social intelligence essential for effective human-machine interaction.

Another example of Type 3 AI, can be found in social robots designed to assist individuals in healthcare settings. These robots, like PARO, a therapeutic robot seal used in elder care facilities, are equipped with sensors and AI algorithms that enable them to perceive human emotions and respond accordingly. PARO recognize human facial expressions and tones of voice, This makes it possible for him to adapt his behavior to provide comfort and companionship to elderly patients.

By understanding and responding to the emotional states of the individuals they interact with, these social robots demonstrate a form of social intelligence, making them valuable tools in enhancing the well-being of patients and providing emotional support in healthcare environments.

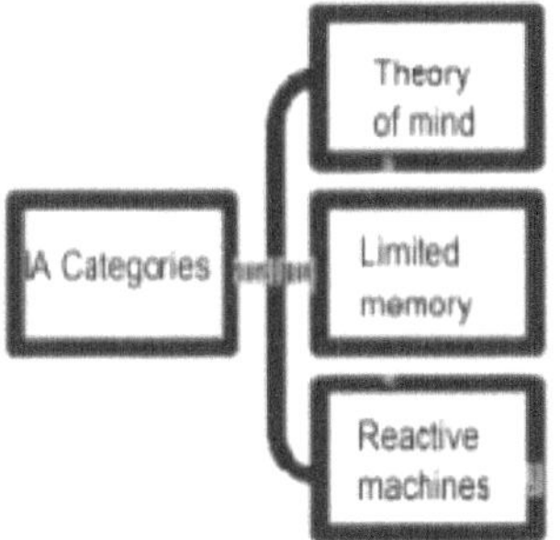

• • • •

AI programming focuses on 'cognitive skills' that include the following:

Learning. This aspect of AI programming focuses on acquiring data and creating rules for how to turn it into actionable information. The rules, which are called algorithms, provide computing devices with step-by-step instructions for how to complete a specific task.

Reasoning. This aspect of AI programming focuses on choosing the right algorithm to reach a desired outcome.

Self-correction. This aspect of AI programming is designed to continually fine-tune algorithms and ensure they provide the most accurate results possible.

Creativity. This aspect of AI uses neural networks, rules-based systems, statistical methods and other AI techniques to generate new images, new text, new music and new ideas.

• • • •

What does "Cognitive Skills" means in the Perspective of Artificial Intelligence?.

In the specific framework of artificial intelligence (AI), "cognitive abilities" are a set of capabilities and processes that are intended to perform and simulate tasks related to people thinking and understanding.

These skills encompass various aspects of people cognition and intelligence, permitting AI systems to perceive, reason, learn and interact with their environment in a manner that mimics human cognitive capabilities.

Cognitive skills are fundamental to creating AI systems that perform tasks requiring human-like thinking and problem-solving abilities. These skills are developed through a combination of algorithms, data, and computational power, and they are central to AI applications across various domains, including healthcare, finance, education, and more.

The development and advancement of cognitive AI systems constitutes an essential part of the broader field of artificial intelligence, which aims to bridge the gap between machines and human intelligence.

Cognitive systems perceive and interpret sensory information from the environment, such as visual, auditory, and tactile data. Computer vision and speech recognition are examples of AI technologies that simulate people perception. AI systems engage in logical reasoning and problem-solving. They evaluate evidence, make inferences, draw conclusions, and follow rules to arrive at decisions or solutions.

Cognitive AI systems have the ability to learn from data and experiences. This includes machine learning techniques that enable models to recognize patterns, adapt to new information, and improve their performance over time; offering a cost-effective complementary alternative to store and retrieve information, this ensures that they are able to preserve context and make use of past experiences when making decisions or providing answers.

Natural language processing (NLP) technologies enable AI systems to understand and generate human language. This includes tasks like language translation, sentiment analysis, and chatbot interactions. Cognitive AI systems are capable of solving complex problems, both in predefined domains (as in expert systems) and in more open-ended, dynamic environments.

Cognitive AI systems understand and adapt to the context in which they operate. This involves comprehending the interests and preferences of users, situational awareness, and adjusting behavior accordingly. Autonomous AI systems are capable of making decisions and taking actions independently, often in real-time or dynamic environments. This is essential for applications like autonomous vehicles and robotics.

They adapt to changing conditions, new data, and evolving circumstances. They modify their behavior or strategies to optimize outcomes. Some AI systems are equipped with the ability to recognize and respond to people emotions, which is valuable in applications like customer service and mental health support.

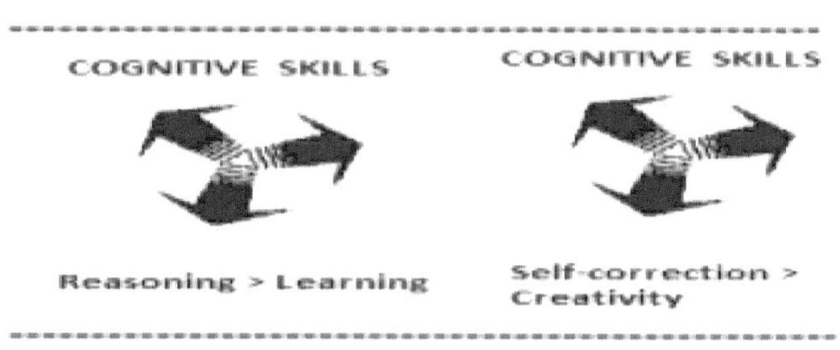

• • • •

Reasoning approaches.

We will illustrate the diverse range of reasoning abilities that AI systems possess, from formal logic and probability to domain-specific expertise and common-sense reasoning. Reasoning is a crucial facet of AI that has the potential to empower machines to make informed decisions and solve complex challenges in a variety of applications and domains.

AI systems work by using formal logic to draw deductions from a set of premises. For instance, if an AI system is given the premises "All humans are mortal" and "Socrates is a human," it use deductive reasoning to conclude that "Socrates is mortal' (Logical).

In probabilistic reasoning, AI systems assess the likelihood of various outcomes based on available evidence and probabilistic models. For example, a recommendation system has the potential to utilise probabilistic reasoning to propose products to a client based on his or her browsing and purchase history.

Expert systems are AI applications that employ rule-based reasoning to provide expert-level advice or make decisions in specific domains. A medical expert system might deploy a set of medical rules and knowledge to diagnose diseases based on the patient's symptoms.

Some AI research focuses on equipping machines with commonsense reasoning capabilities that equip them to make more intuitive and context-aware decisions. For instance, an AI assistant may use common-sense reasoning to answer user questions like, 'Can I fit an elephant in my refrigerator?'.

Abductive reasoning consists of inferring the most probable explanation or hypothesis for a set of observations. For example, in diagnostic systems, abductive reasoning is used to determine the underlying cause of symptoms when multiple diagnoses are possible.

AI systems rationalise about events and actions over time. For instance, in a scheduling application, the system optimise a sequence of tasks while respecting time constraints by using temporal reasoning.

AI systems analyze cause-and-effect relationships to understand the impact of actions or events. In healthcare, causal reasoning may be used to identify the factors contributing to a patient's health condition. Analogical reasoning attempts to draw parallels between different situations or domains. For example, an AI system might utilise analogical reasoning to transfer knowledge from one problem domain to another.

Inductive reasoning consists of making generalizations based on specific observations or data. Machine learning algorithms, such as decision trees or neural networks, use inductive reasoning to make predictions based on training data.

With inductive reasoning, we make observations to reach a conclusion. This skill is useful in making predictions and creating generalizations. Our conclusion may not always be true, but it should be reasonable based on the evidence.

For example, we notice that customers have bought more of your product during the third quarter of the year for the past three years. Based on that information, we predict that your customers will buy more of our product during the third quarter of the coming year and we increase production to be prepared.

Inductive reasoning is different from deductive reasoning. With deductive reasoning, we start with a generalization or theory and then test it by applying it to specific incidents. Deductive reasoning is using general ideas to reach a specific conclusion. Inductive reasoning uses specific ideas to reach a broad conclusion

Scientists may use deductive reasoning to test a hypothesis in a lab. Many law enforcement, military, or corporate leaders must be able to use inductive reasoning by taking a quick sweep of a situation and making a vital, time-sensitive decision. Inductive reasoning allows individuals to accurately see the signs of something bigger at play.

Constraint reasoning is used in optimization problems, where AI systems find solutions that satisfy a set of constraints. For example, a logistics system may use constraint reasoning to plan delivery routes that minimize costs and meet delivery time constraints.

• • • • •

INDUCTIVE REASONING	DEDUCTIVE REASONING
Using specific observations to reach a broad conclusion	Using general ideas to reach a specific conclusion.
Used in law enforcement to narrow down suspects	Used in science to reach a hypothesis

• • • •

'Logical Reasoning' in the AI context.

Logical reasoning (LR) is a powerful tool in AI for solving complex problems, making decisions based on explicit rules, and ensuring the correctness of algorithms and systems. While AI encompasses various approaches and techniques, logical reasoning remains a foundational component, especially in knowledge-based systems and formal reasoning tasks.

Logical reasoning encompasses the application of formal logic, deductive reasoning and mathematical principles to draw conclusions, make inferences and solve problems. LR in AI often relies on symbolic logic, which represents knowledge and statements using symbols, variables, and logical operators like AND, OR, NOT, and IF-THEN. Propositional logic and predicate logic are commonly used formalisms.

Deductive reasoning is a form of logical reasoning where specific conclusions are drawn from general premises or axioms. In AI, expert systems and theorem provers use deductive reasoning to make decisions based on predefined rules.

Inference engines are components of AI systems that perform logical inference. They apply rules, evaluate conditions, and determine the validity of statements to reach logical conclusions. These engines are commonly used in expert systems.

In AI, logical reasoning often involves representing knowledge in a structured and formal way. Knowledge bases store facts, rules, and relationships in a format that is amenable to logical reasoning.

Rule-based systems, also known as rule-based reasoning or expert systems, use sets of logical rules (if-then statements) to make decisions or solve problems in specific domains. For example, a medical expert system may use rules to diagnose diseases based on patient symptoms.

Automated reasoning refers to the process of using computer algorithms to perform logical reasoning and prove theorems. This is crucial in fields like formal verification of software and hardware systems. Mathematical logic, including propositional and first-order logic, is used in AI to model and reason about complex systems, particularly in areas like automated theorem proving and formal methods.

Fuzzy logic extends classical Boolean logic to handle uncertainty and imprecision. It's used in control systems and decision-making processes where precise values may not be available (The law of noncontradiction asserts that a proposition can not be true and false at the same time).

. . . .

$$x + y = y + x$$
$$z\,(x + y) = zx + zy$$
$$x - y = y + x$$
$$z(x - y) = zx - zy$$

> The grammatical form of a sentence doesn't necessarily match with its logical form. The common sense that comes from the natural language can be misleading about the formal content of a statement (Boolean logic).

While logical reasoning is often associated with deduction, inductive logic involves making generalizations from specific observations. Machine learning algorithms, such as decision trees and neural networks, use inductive reasoning to generalize from data. Logical reasoning is applied in a wide range of AI applications, including natural language processing, robotics, automated planning, game playing (e.g., chess and Go), knowledge-based systems, and formal verification of software.

Advancing the field of AI to perform common-sense reasoning—drawing conclusions based on everyday knowledge and context—is a challenging research area. It aims to imbue AI with human-like reasoning abilities. Logical reasoning often leads AI systems to provide explanations for their decisions, which is essential for building trust and transparency in AI applications.

. . . .

Probabilistic Reasoning.

Probabilistic reasoning concerns modeling and reasoning under conditions of uncertainty using probability theory. It provides a way for AI systems to make decisions, draw inferences, and assess the likelihood of various outcomes when dealing with incomplete or noisy information.

Probabilistic reasoning is a powerful tool in AI because it presents an alternative to the systems to make informed decisions and predictions in situations where information is incomplete, noisy, or uncertain. It is particularly valuable in domains where uncertainty is prevalent and where the consequences of decisions are significant.

Probabilistic reasoning is employed in AI to deal with situations where there is uncertainty or incomplete information. This is common in real-world applications where not all data is precise or known. Probabilistic reasoning relies on probability theory, which provides a mathematical framework for representing and manipulating uncertainty. Key concepts include probability distributions, conditional probabilities, and Bayesian reasoning.

Bayesian networks (or Bayesian belief networks) are a popular graphical model used for probabilistic reasoning. They consist of nodes representing random variables and edges representing probabilistic dependencies between variables. Bayesian networks are used for tasks such as risk assessment, medical diagnosis, and decision support.

MDPs are used in reinforcement learning, a subfield of AI, to model decision-making under uncertainty. Agents employ MDPs to make sequential decisions while considering the probabilistic outcomes of their actions.

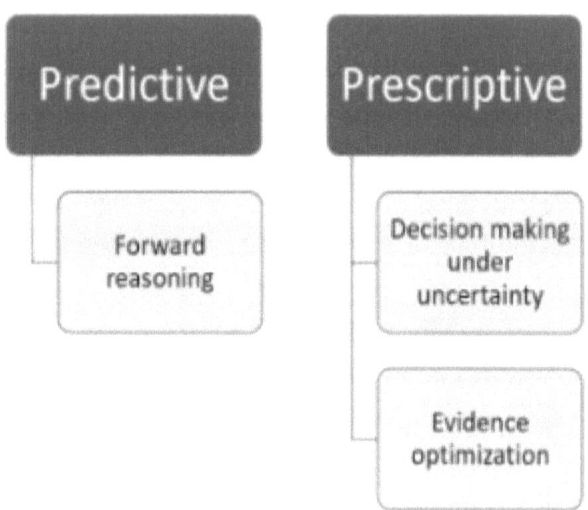

Monte Carlo methods, including Monte Carlo simulation and sampling, are used to approximate probabilistic quantities by generating random samples. These methods are often used in Bayesian inference and decision analysis. HMMs are probabilistic models used for sequence data analysis. They are employed in speech recognition, natural language processing, and bioinformatics for tasks like part-of-speech tagging and speech-to-text conversion.

Probability distributions

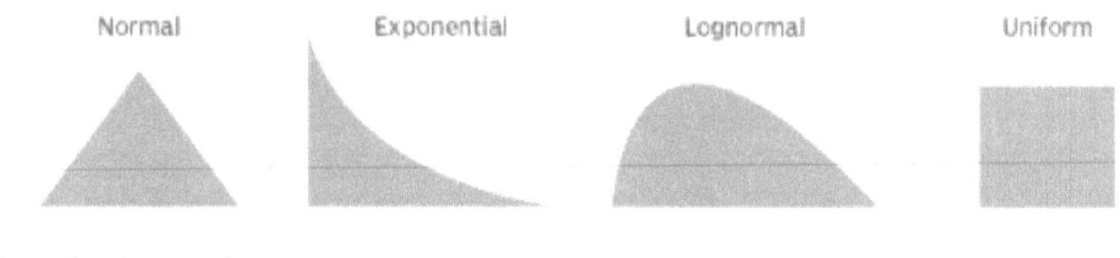

Source: bayesian.networks

• • • •

Probabilistic programming languages (PPLs) enable the creation of probabilistic models on the basis of programming constructs. PPLs make it easier to express complex probabilistic models and perform probabilistic inference. Many machine learning algorithms incorporate probabilistic reasoning. For example, Gaussian Naive Bayes uses probability distributions to classify data, and probabilistic graphical models like Conditional Random Fields are utilised for structured prediction tasks.

Probabilistic reasoning has applications in diverse fields, including healthcare (disease diagnosis and prognosis), finance (risk assessment and portfolio management), autonomous vehicles (decision-making under uncertainty), natural language processing (speech recognition and machine translation), and robotics (robot localization and mapping).

Probabilistic reasoning is central to decision-making processes where the goal is to choose actions or make predictions that maximize expected utility or minimize expected loss while considering uncertainty.

In risk analysis, probabilistic reasoning helps assess and manage uncertainty by quantifying the probabilities of different outcomes and their associated risks. In predictive analytics, probabilistic models are be considered to estimate future events or trends based on historical data and probabilistic assumptions.

· · · ·

Common Sense Reasoning.

· · · ·

Common sense reasoning remains an active and evolving area of AI research, as it represents one of the key challenges in building AI systems that interact with people in a natural and intuitive manner. Progress in this field has the potential to greatly enhance the capabilities of AI across various applications and domains.

Common sense (CS) is about broad and fundamental knowledge and reasoning abilities that humans typically possess, often acquired through life experience and cultural context. It includes basic understanding of the physical world, social norms, causality, and relationships.

CS is challenging for AI because it involves making inferences and judgments about situations that are not explicitly stated in data. AI systems need to fill in the gaps and make educated guesses based on context and general knowledge. In principle, this is not an easy thing to achieve for the engine.

This is a popular benchmark in the AI community that tests an AI system's ability to resolve pronoun ambiguity using common sense. It consists of a set of sentences where the meaning of a pronoun depends on background knowledge and context.

Some AI approaches use structured knowledge bases to store and access common sense knowledge. These knowledge bases contain facts and relationships that represent general knowledge about the world. Ontologies are formal representations of concepts and their relationships, often used to encode common sense knowledge. They provide a structured way to represent domain-independent information.

AI systems designed for common sense reasoning often incorporate reasoning engines that utilise logic, inference rules, and semantic networks to make inferences based on available knowledge. Some AI researchers explore machine learning techniques to acquire and apply common sense knowledge.

Common sense reasoning is crucial in applications where AI interacts with people, such as chatbots, virtual assistants, and autonomous systems. It helps AI systems understand user queries, provide meaningful responses, and navigate real-world scenarios.

Evaluating the performance of common sense reasoning systems can be challenging because it often relies on qualitative assessments of whether the system's responses align with people intuition. Ensuring the robustness of common sense reasoning models is an ongoing research challenge.

Organizations like OpenAI have been working on advancing common sense reasoning in AI. They have created benchmarks and competitions, such as the OpenAI Commonsense Reasoning Challenge, to encourage the development of AI systems with better common sense reasoning abilities.

Common sense reasoning covers the ability of AI systems to possess and implement general knowledge, intuition and everyday reasoning capabilities similar to those of people. This type of reasoning aims to enable AI to make sense of the world and respond intelligently to a wide range of situations that may not be explicitly covered in training data.

Advancing common sense reasoning is a critical step toward building more human-like and capable AI systems. Research in this area aims to improve AI's ability to understand and navigate complex, real-world situations and provide more contextually relevant responses.

After all, it is language, not logical forms, through which people acquire knowledge about the world. Thus, in order to match the scale and complexity of human-level knowledge acquisition, AI cannot go far without direct integration of language.

Again, the switch to language-based formalisms is the key to benefit from the empirical breakthroughs of deep neural networks, as it facilitates powerful learning by transferring linguistic models to knowledge models.

AI requires rethinking and challenging some of the most fundamental assumptions in the current paradigms of machine learning and AI. It also challenges our conceptual understanding about knowledge, reasoning, and language.

However, human-level intuitive inferences require complex compositional reasoning over diverse concepts, including objects, actions, locations, attributes, and emotions. In other words, the space of concepts is infinite, as concepts can be composed of other concepts recursively.

The reasoning framework, to be practically useful, should be ready to cover the full spectrum of concepts and compositions of concepts that we encounter in our everyday physical and social interactions with the world. In addition, the real world is filled with previously unseen situations, which require creative generation of hypotheses, novel compositions of concepts, and novel discovery of reasoning rules.

Within the AI logic research communities, language has been very rarely or only minimally integrated into reasoning, as prior research aimed to operate on top of logic-based formalisms detached from natural language. In contrast, within natural language processing (NLP) research communities, a subfield of AI that focuses on human language technologies, questions about intuitive reasoning, common-sense reasoning.

$$\bullet \ \bullet \ \bullet \ \bullet$$

Analogical Reasoning.

$$\bullet \ \bullet \ \bullet \ \bullet$$

Analogical reasoning in the context of artificial intelligence (AI) designates the ability of AI systems to recognize and apply analogies or similarities between different situations, domains, or concepts. It involves finding relationships, patterns, and similarities between entities or ideas and using these relationships to draw inferences, make predictions, or solve problems.

Efforts to advance analogical reasoning in AI aim to improve the ability of AI systems to generalize knowledge, adapt to new situations, and engage in more creative problem-solving. These developments have the potential to enhance AI's capacity to learn and reason across various domains and contribute to more intelligent and versatile AI applications. AI systems to transfer knowledge from one context to another.

An analogy is a comparison between two or more entities or situations that highlights their similarities in certain respects while ignoring differences. It is often expressed in the form "A is to B as C is to D," where A, B, C, and D are entities or concepts.

Analogical reasoning is a key aspect of human cognition and intelligence. It enables humans to learn from past experiences, solve novel problems, and make connections between seemingly unrelated ideas. In AI, replicating this ability is crucial for creative problem-solving and knowledge transfer.

One classic example of analogical reasoning is the analogy between "the human heart is to the circulatory system as the engine is to a car." This analogy highlights the role of the heart in pumping blood through the circulatory system, similar to how the engine powers a car.

• • • •

Analogical reasoning is often used in natural language processing (NLP) tasks. For instance, word embeddings and vector representations of words can capture semantic relationships and analogies. For example, the relationship between "king" and "queen" can be represented as an analogy: "king - queen ≈ man - woman."

Analogical reasoning is closely related to common sense reasoning, as it involves applying general knowledge and principles to new situations. Common sense knowledge often includes analogies and metaphors that help in understanding and reasoning about the world.

Analogical reasoning has played a significant role in scientific discoveries. Scientists often draw analogies between phenomena in different domains to formulate hypotheses and develop new theories.

It is discussed that analogical reasoning typically relies on the identification and transfer of structural elements from a known system (the source) to a new and relatively unfamiliar system (the target). Two different types of reasoning are considered and some of the psychological processes implicated in their identification are examined.

It is therefore considered that the productive use of analogy, namely the utilisation of analogy to produce new knowledge on the explanatory structure of the target system, rather than on the similarity in its structure, since the relevant structure of the target system is not known.

AI systems use analogical reasoning in various ways, such as in case-based reasoning, where past cases are used to solve new problems by finding analogies between cases. AI also employ analogies for transfer learning, where knowledge learned in one domain is applied to another domain.

Analogical reasoning remains a challenging problem in AI because it requires identifying relevant similarities and transferring knowledge effectively. Building AI systems that perform analogical reasoning at a human-like level is an ongoing research area.

Analogical reasoning has applications in recommendation systems, knowledge representation and reasoning, creative problem-solving, scientific discovery, and education, among others. Some AI models and systems use analogy-based learning to acquire new knowledge by recognizing analogies between known facts and new information.

Emotion Recognition.

'Emotion recognition' in the context of artificial intelligence entails the ability of machines to detect and interpret people emotions based on various cues, such as facial expressions, speech, text, and physiological signals.

These examples will demonstrate how 'emotion recognition' technologies may be applied in a variety of fields, from healthcare and mental well-being to customer service and entertainment. 'Emotion recognition' capabilities in AI aim to improve people-computer interactions and enhance the understanding of user emotions, leading to more personalized and responsive AI systems.

• • • •

Feature Type	Feature Description
Width	Left eye Right eye Mouth
Height	Right eye Left eye Right eye Mouth
Distance	Left and right eyes Eyes to brows Eyes to mouth Eyes and nose Nose and mouth
Angle	Left eye with right eye and mouth Right Eye with left eye and mouth Mouth with both eyes Mouth with both eyes

Visible Features. Sciencedirect.com

• • • •

AI systems equipped with computer vision technology are able to analyze facial expressions in real-time to identify emotions. For instance: In video conferencing tools, emotion recognition will be used to assess participants' engagement and mood during virtual meetings.

In market research, analyzing customer reactions to advertisements by tracking facial expressions helps gauge emotional responses to the content. AI models analyze the tone, pitch, and speech patterns in people voices to determine emotions.

In customer service, voice assistants and chatbots recognize frustration or anger in a customer's voice and adapt their responses accordingly. In mental health applications, 'emotion recognition' from speech assist therapists in monitoring patients' emotional states during therapy sessions.

Natural language processing (NLP) techniques enable AI systems to analyze text data, such as social media posts or customer reviews, to detect emotional content.

Social media platforms use emotion recognition to understand user sentiment and tailor

content recommendations or targeted advertising. Customer support chatbots gauge customer satisfaction and respond empathetically to user inquiries based on their expressed emotions in text messages.

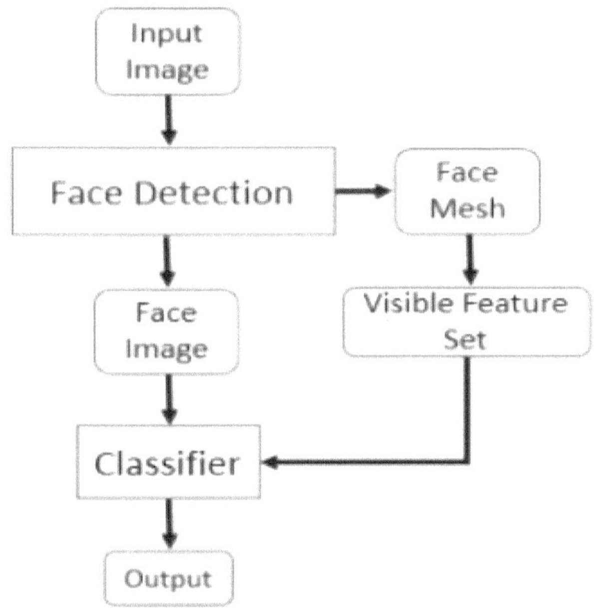

Proposed emotion recognition model architecture

Source: sciencedirect.com

AI systems utilize physiological signals, such as heart rate variability and skin conductance, to infer emotional states.

Emotion Recognition in Mental Health Monitoring.

Scenario: A mental health monitoring system employs wearable devices integrated with AI algorithms to track physiological signals and infer the emotional well-being of individuals.

Individuals wear smartwatches or health monitoring devices equipped with sensors capable of measuring physiological signals such as heart rate variability (HRV) and skin conductance. The wearable devices continuously collect physiological data throughout the day, recording variations in heart rate and skin conductance levels.

AI algorithms process the collected physiological signals to extract meaningful patterns. For example, they analyze the time intervals between heartbeats (HRV) and changes in skin conductance.

The AI system employs a machine learning model trained on a diverse dataset to associate patterns in physiological signals with different emotional states. The model learns to recognize typical patterns corresponding to emotions such as stress, relaxation, excitement, or calmness.

In real-time, the AI system continuously analyzes the incoming physiological data from the wearable devices. It compares the patterns observed with those stored in its database to make predictions about the individual's emotional state.

Based on the inferred emotional state, the system provides personalized feedback or alerts. For instance, if heightened stress levels are detected, the system may suggest relaxation exercises, mindfulness activities, or prompt the individual to take a break.

The system detect changes in emotional states early, allowing for timely intervention or support, especially in individuals dealing with stress, anxiety, or mood disorders.

By continuously adapting to the individual's physiological responses, the AI system provides personalized recommendations for emotional well-being, promoting a tailored approach to mental health support.

The continuous nature of physiological signal monitoring enables the system to track emotional trends over time, providing valuable insights for long-term mental health assessment and intervention.

• • • •

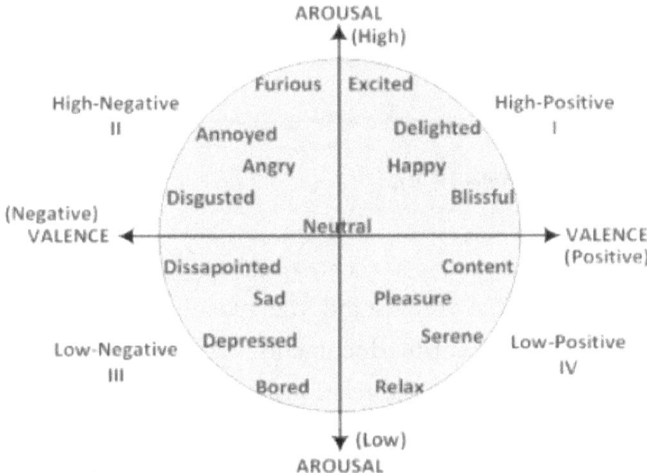

Wearable devices with emotion recognition capabilities empower users to manage stress by providing real-time feedback on their emotional responses. In education, physiological sensors detect students' frustration levels during learning activities, resulting in personalised interventions.

'Emotion recognition' is improving people computer interactions by enabling systems to adapt to users' emotional states. Emotion-aware video games adjust gameplay and challenges based on players' emotions, providing a more engaging experience. Virtual assistants respond with empathy and emotional intelligence when they detect users are upset or stressed.

Can be applied in security settings to identify potential threats or abnormal behavior. At airports or public venues, 'emotion recognition' technology identifies individuals exhibiting signs of distress or suspicious behavior. In driver monitoring systems, it detect signs of drowsiness or distraction and trigger safety alerts.

1.1. Key Aspects of 'Natural Language Understanding'

Semantic Understanding.

• • • •

NLU systems aim to understand the meaning of words, phrases, sentences, and even entire documents. This includes recognizing synonyms, antonyms, and the relationships between words. Semantic understanding in NLU systems goes beyond mere word recognition. It penetrates into contextual interpretation, where the system comprehends words within the framework of the sentences they are used in.

This calls for an appreciation not just the dictionary definition of words, but also their connotations and implications in a specific context. For instance, in the sentence, "He plays a mean guitar," understanding the word "mean" requires recognizing it as a colloquial term for exceptional rather than its more common definition denoting unpleasantness.

NLU systems engage in syntactic analysis to grasp the grammatical structure of sentences. This presupposes an understanding of the roles that different words play in a sentence, such as subject, verb, object, and so forth.

By comprehending the syntactic structure, the system discern the relationships between words and interpret the intended meaning accurately. For instance, in the sentence, "The cat chased the dog," the system needs to recognize that the cat is the one doing the chasing, and the dog is the one being chased.

Beyond syntax and semantics, NLU systems also focus on pragmatic understanding. Pragmatics deals with the study of language meaning in context. The aim is to understand the implicit meanings, indirect speech acts, and the speaker's intentions.

This level of understanding is crucial in interpreting statements where the literal meaning might not align with the intended message. For instance, understanding the difference between "Can you pass the salt?" as a request and "Could you pass the salt?" as a more polite request involves pragmatic analysis.

Semantic understanding extends to recognizing sentiments expressed in text. NLU systems employ sentiment analysis techniques to determine the emotional tone of a piece of text, whether it's positive, negative, or neutral. This capability is invaluable in applications like social media monitoring, customer feedback analysis, and brand sentiment tracking. Understanding the sentiment behind words allows these systems to gauge public opinion and respond effectively.

Semantic understanding also encompasses recognizing named entities within text, such as names of people, places, organizations, and dates. NER is crucial for tasks like information retrieval, question answering systems, and language translation. By identifying and categorizing named entities, NLU systems provide more relevant and accurate responses to user queries.

Example: Social Media Monitoring for a Brand Imagine a company wants to monitor social media posts to understand how people perceive their new product, a smartphone called "TechX." By employing NER techniques, an NLU system analyze social media posts and identify named entities, such as product names, in the following post:

"Just bought the new TechX phone! It's amazing and totally worth the hype. #TechX #NewGadget" In this example, the NLU system recognizes the named entity "TechX" as the product name. This understanding is crucial for the company because it helps them track mentions of their product accurately in a vast sea of social media data.

By analyzing numerous such posts, the company gauge the sentiment associated with the product, understand popular features, and even identify potential issues that customers might be discussing.

Semantic understanding, particularly through NER, empowers businesses to sift through massive amounts of unstructured data, extracting valuable insights. In this case, the company assess the overall public sentiment, identify key influencers, and promptly respond to both positive and negative feedback, leading to informed marketing strategies and improved customer satisfaction.

Example of semantic understanding in sentiment analysis for customer feedback:

Customer Feedback Analysis for an E-commerce Platform Imagine an e-commerce platform receives the following customer review: "The product arrived on time, but the packaging was damaged. However, customer service was quick to respond and resolve the issue. I appreciate their prompt assistance."

Semantic understanding, particularly in the form of sentiment analysis, permits the NLU system to decipher the nuanced emotions in this feedback.

In this case:

Contextual Interpretation: The system understands that the customer is praising the prompt response of the customer service team despite the initial issue with the damaged packaging.

Syntactic Analysis: The system recognizes the syntactic structure of the sentence, identifying the different components such as the timely delivery, damaged packaging, and positive customer service experience.

Pragmatic Understanding: The system comprehends the pragmatic elements of the review. Despite the negative aspect of the damaged packaging, the customer's overall sentiment is positive due to the efficient resolution by customer service.

Sentiment Analysis: The system identifies the mixed sentiment in the feedback, where the negative sentiment regarding the damaged packaging is outweighed by the positive sentiment towards the customer service, resulting in an overall positive sentiment score.

This semantic understanding enables the e-commerce platform to not only acknowledge the specific issues faced by the customer but also recognize and appreciate the effectiveness of their customer service team. By analyzing a large volume of such feedback, the platform identify patterns, address common pain points, and enhance customer service protocols, leading to improved customer satisfaction and loyalty.

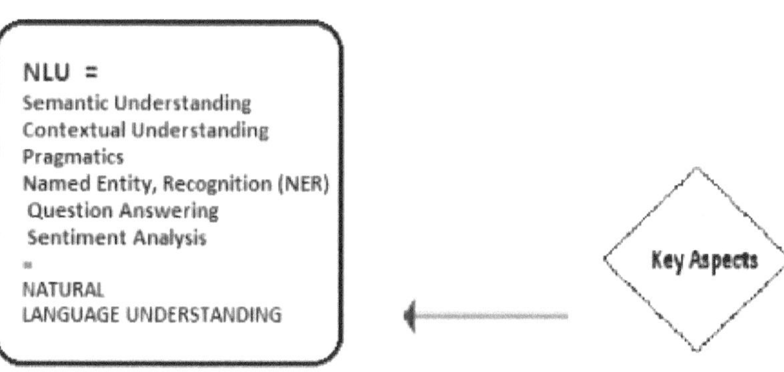

Example of semantic understanding in the context of news articles and information retrieval:

News Article Summarization for a Media Outlet.

Imagine a news organization wants to automate the process of summarizing news articles for their online readers. Semantic understanding, particularly in the form of contextual interpretation and named entity recognition, plays a vital role in achieving this task.

Consider the following news article snippet:

"Scientists at XYZ University have made a groundbreaking discovery in the field of renewable energy. Their research, published in the prestigious Journal of Energy Innovations, reveals a new method of harnessing solar power efficiently. The team, led by Dr. Sarah Johnson, has developed a prototype solar panel that has shown a 30% increase in energy conversion rates compared to traditional models."

Semantic Understanding in Action:

Contextual Interpretation: The NLU system understands the context of the article, recognizing that it discusses a significant scientific breakthrough in renewable energy, specifically in the field of solar power.

Named Entity Recognition (NER): The system identifies key entities such as the university (XYZ University), the publication (Journal of Energy Innovations), the researcher (Dr. Sarah Johnson), and the specific achievement (30% increase in energy conversion rates).

Contextual Analysis: By understanding the relationships between these entities and the context in which they are mentioned, the system comprehends that Dr. Sarah Johnson and her team at XYZ University are responsible for the groundbreaking discovery, and the results were published in a reputable journal.

Utilizing semantic understanding, the news organization's system generate concise and accurate summaries for their readers. For instance:

"Researchers at XYZ University, led by Dr. Sarah Johnson, have developed a prototype solar panel that boosts energy conversion rates by 30%, a breakthrough detailed in the Journal of Energy Innovations."

This summary captures the essence of the original article, providing readers with the most crucial information in a condensed and comprehensible form. Semantic understanding allows automated systems to process vast amounts of textual data, distill essential information, and present it in a meaningful way for users, enhancing their overall reading experience.

• • • •

Contextual Understanding.

• • • •

NLU systems consider the context in which language is used. Words or phrases have different meanings based on the surrounding text. Understanding context is crucial for accurate interpretation. Contextual understanding in NLU systems implies analyzing words and phrases within the context of surrounding text to determine their accurate meanings.

Words have multiple meanings depending on the context in which they are utilised. For instance, the word "bank" refer to a financial institution or the side of a river. By analyzing the words and phrases around it, NLU systems discern the intended meaning. For example, in the sentence "He deposited money in the bank," the context suggests that "bank" refers to a financial institution.

One of the challenges in language processing is dealing with ambiguities. Words often have multiple meanings, and sentences are structured in ways that lead to different interpretations. Contextual understanding allows NLU systems to resolve these ambiguities by considering the broader context.

For instance, in the sentence "She saw the man with the telescope," the word "saw" could mean either visually observed or met socially. The presence of the word "telescope" clarifies the meaning, indicating that the woman observed the man using a telescope.

Contextual understanding also includes resolving pronouns and other expressions that point to previously mentioned entities (coreference resolution). For example, in the sentence "John called Mary because he wanted to invite her to the party," understanding that "he" refers to John and "her" refers to Mary requires considering the context of the conversation. NLU systems use contextual clues to link pronouns to their appropriate antecedents, ensuring a coherent interpretation of the text.

Understanding the context goes beyond just the immediate sentence. NLU systems also consider temporal and spatial context. Temporal context involves understanding the timeline of events mentioned in the text. For instance, in a news article, understanding the sequence of events is crucial for comprehending the story accurately.

Spatial context is about understanding the physical locations mentioned in the text. This is particularly important in tasks like mapping services and navigation systems where understanding locations and their relationships is essential.

Contextual understanding also extends to cultural nuances and domain-specific knowledge. Different cultures may use language differently, including idiomatic expressions and colloquialisms. Additionally, different domains (such as legal, medical, or scientific) have specialized terminology. NLU systems need to consider these cultural and domain-specific contexts to interpret language accurately within the appropriate cultural or professional context.

By analyzing the surrounding text, resolving ambiguities, handling coreference, considering temporal and spatial context, and accounting for cultural and domain specific nuances, NLU systems provide more precise and contextually relevant interpretations of text, enabling a wide range of applications from chatbots to machine translation and information retrieval systems.

Example in the context of cultural nuances and domain-specific knowledge.

Cultural Nuances and Domain-Specific Context in Language Understanding.

Context: A Conversation Between Colleagues from Different Cultural Backgrounds in a Medical Setting.

Scenario:

John, a doctor from the United States, is discussing a patient's condition with Mei, a doctor from China, who is not as fluent in English.

Dialogue:

John: "The patient seems to be in low spirits today."

Mei: "Low spirits? What do you mean?"

John: "I mean the patient appears to be emotionally down and lacks enthusiasm."

In this example, the phrase "low spirits" represents a cultural nuance. While commonly used in English, it might not directly translate into other languages, and its meaning could be ambiguous, especially when idiomatic expressions are involved.

Domain-Specific Knowledge:

Consider a medical conversation between two doctors, one specializing in cardiology and the other in neurology:

Scenario:

Dr. Smith (Cardiologist): "The patient has been complaining of chest pain and shortness of breath."

Dr. Johnson (Neurologist): "Is there any numbness or tingling sensation accompanying the chest pain?"

In this scenario, the discussion involves domain-specific knowledge. The terms "chest pain" and "shortness of breath" are common in the medical field but might have different interpretations when discussed outside of a medical context. Additionally, the mention of "numbness" and "tingling sensation" is specific to neurology and might not be immediately understood by someone without medical expertise.

Cultural Nuances and Domain-Specific Context in Interpretation.

In both scenarios, contextual understanding is vital. In the first scenario, Mei might not be familiar with the idiomatic expression "low spirits." Through the context of the conversation, especially John's explanation, she understand that this is the patient's emotional state.

In the second scenario, both doctors understand the specific medical terms and symptoms within their domain of expertise. Their discussion relies heavily on this shared knowledge, ensuring accurate communication about the patient's condition.

Understanding these cultural nuances and domain-specific contexts is crucial in diverse and specialized fields such as healthcare. It ensures that communication is precise, avoiding misunderstandings that could lead to misdiagnoses or misinterpretations of a patient's condition. In broader applications, such nuanced understanding is valuable in various industries where language and context intersect, such as legal, scientific, and technical fields.

Example involving cultural nuances and domain-specific context in the context of technology and software development.

Cross-Cultural Software Development Team Meeting.

Context: A Virtual Meeting Among Software Developers from Different Cultural Backgrounds.

Scenario: Sarah, a software developer from the United States, is leading a virtual team meeting with developers from India, Japan, and Brazil. The team is discussing the implementation of a new feature in their software product.

Dialogue:

Sarah: "We need to refactor this module to enhance its performance. Let's use a microservices architecture for better scalability."

Kiran (from India): "Microservices? I'm not sure I understand. Can you elaborate?"

Yuki (from Japan): "I think I get it. We break down the module into smaller services, right?"

Carlos (from Brazil): "Is this similar to what we call service-oriented architecture?'.

Cultural Nuances and Domain-Specific Context in Interpretation. Different cultures might have varying ways of approaching and conceptualizing software architecture. While Sarah uses the term "microservices," Kiran might not be immediately familiar with this term, as it could be a relatively new concept in their local tech industry jargon. By Sarah elaborating on the concept, taking into account the diverse cultural backgrounds of her team members, she ensures everyone is on the same page.

Software development terminologies also vary within the industry. Yuki's understanding aligns with the concept Sarah described, showcasing his familiarity with modern software architecture principles.

Carlos brings up the term "service-oriented architecture," indicating his awareness of a related concept. Sarah needs to bridge these different terms, emphasizing the similarities while highlighting the specific advantages of microservices for their project.

Resolution and Collaboration:

Understanding these cultural nuances and domain-specific contexts allows the team to collaborate effectively. Sarah takes the time to explain the concept of microservices in a way that resonates with the diverse perspectives in her team.

By acknowledging the varying levels of familiarity with specific terms and ensuring everyone comprehends the chosen approach, the team work cohesively towards the successful implementation of the new software feature. This inclusive communication approach fosters a collaborative atmosphere, leveraging the strengths of each team member's background and expertise.

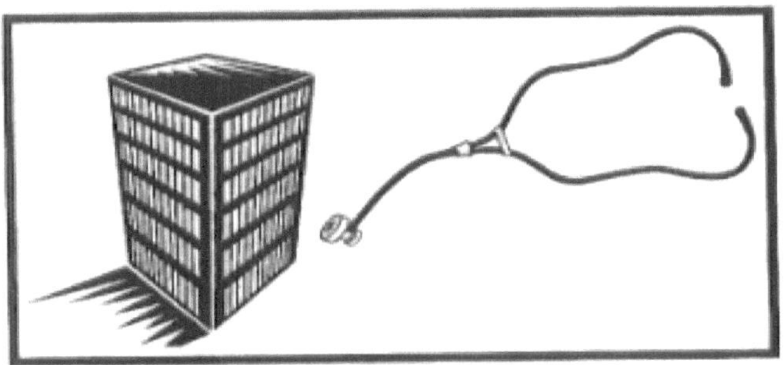

· · · ·

Pragmatics.

· · · ·

NLU systems attempt to grasp the intended meaning behind a statement, considering factors like sarcasm, humor, and implied information. This is important for understanding the speaker's true intention. Pragmatics in NLU is the interpretation of language in context, understanding not just the literal meanings of words and sentences but also the implied meanings.

Consider the sentence, "I'm freezing" said on a warm day. The literal meaning indicates feeling extremely cold, but pragmatically, it could imply the speaker is feeling too cold due to air conditioning, suggesting discomfort.

Pragmatic understanding is vital for recognizing sarcasm and irony, where the intended meaning contradicts the literal words. For example, if someone says, "Great job!" in a sarcastic tone after a mistake, the NLU system needs to pick up on the tone and context to grasp the true negative intention behind the words.

Humor often relies on wordplay, double meanings, or unexpected twists in language. Pragmatic analysis helps NLU systems understand jokes and witty remarks. For instance, in a pun like "I used to be a baker because I kneaded dough," the wordplay on "kneaded" relies on pragmatic interpretation for the humor to be grasped.

Sometimes, what is not said is as important as what is said. Pragmatics deals with implied information or implicatures. If someone says, "I ate some cake," it implies they didn't eat all the cake. NLU systems need to understand these implicatures to comprehend the speaker's complete message accurately.

Pragmatic analysis also demands an understanding of polite language and indirect requests. For example, a request like "Could you pass the salt?" is more polite than the direct imperative form "Pass the salt." Pragmatics helps NLU systems discern the politeness level and the intended request in such statements. Pragmatic understanding is heavily influenced by cultural and social context.

Different cultures have unique norms regarding politeness, humor, and indirect communication. NLU systems need to consider these cultural nuances to accurately interpret statements. What might be considered humorous in one culture could be perceived as offensive in another.

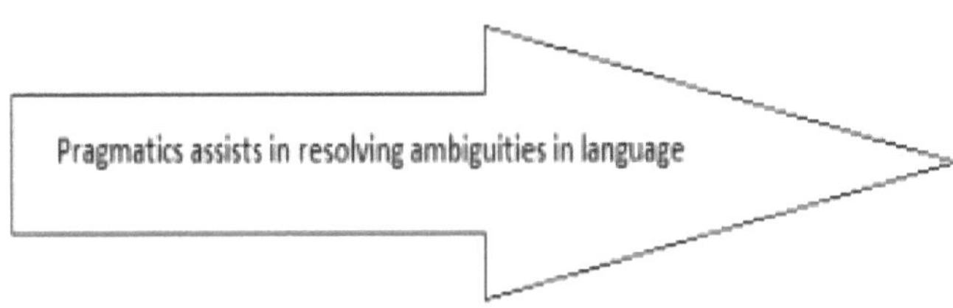

When a sentence has multiple possible interpretations, pragmatics helps in selecting the most contextually appropriate one. This is crucial for tasks like machine translation and dialogue systems where ambiguous statements are common.

Example: Ambiguity Resolution in Customer Service.

Context: A Customer Service Chatbot Interaction.

Scenario:

A customer, Alex, is chatting with a customer service chatbot to inquire about the delivery of a product.

Dialogue:

Chatbot: "When will my order arrive?"

Alex: "Can you check the status of my order?"

Chatbot: "Certainly, I can help you with that. Please provide your order number."

Alex: "It's 12345."

Chatbot: "Thank you. Your order will arrive tomorrow."

In this scenario, the phrase "your order will arrive tomorrow" contains an ambiguity. It's unclear whether the delivery will happen tomorrow, or if the chatbot means the order will be dispatched tomorrow and arrive on a later date.

Pragmatic Ambiguity Resolution.

Understanding the pragmatic context is essential to resolve this ambiguity. If the chatbot intends to communicate the delivery date, it needs to consider the customer's likely interpretation. Since Alex's query was about the delivery time, the pragmatic interpretation should be the delivery date.

The chatbot, equipped with pragmatics, should clarify further to remove the ambiguity. For instance: Chatbot: "Your order is scheduled to be delivered tomorrow, on [specific date]."

By providing the specific delivery date, the chatbot resolves the ambiguity and ensures that the customer understands the precise information. Pragmatic understanding in this context involves recognizing the ambiguity, inferring the customer's intention, and responding in a way that aligns with the customer's likely interpretation of the query.

In customer service interactions, especially in written communication where tone of voice and facial expressions are absent, pragmatics plays a vital role in ensuring that the customer's queries are understood correctly and that the responses are clear, accurate, and contextually appropriate.

Example: Ambiguity Resolution in Language Translation.

Context: A Language Translation Application.

Scenario:

A user, Maria, is using a language translation app to translate a sentence from English to French.

Dialogue:

Maria: "Translate the word 'bank' to French."

Translation App: "Banque."

Maria's request can be interpreted in two ways: she might be asking for the translation of the English word "bank" to French, or she might be asking for the French word for a financial institution. This ambiguity arises from the multiple meanings of the word "bank."

Pragmatic Ambiguity Resolution.

Understanding the context and user intent is crucial for resolving this ambiguity. In this case, the translation app needs to recognize that Maria is most likely asking for the translation of the English word "bank" to French. By considering the pragmatic context, the app provides the translation based on the word Maria provided.

Translation App: "The translation of 'bank' to French is 'banque.'"

By clarifying the specific word Maria wanted to translate and providing the appropriate response, the translation app resolves the ambiguity. Pragmatic understanding helps the app discern the user's intent, ensuring accurate and contextually relevant translations in multilingual communication scenarios.

Example: Ambiguity Resolution in Virtual Assistant Responses.

Context: A Conversation with a Virtual Assistant.

Scenario:

User: "Set up a meeting with Mark." The user's command, "Set up a meeting with Mark," contains an ambiguity. It's unclear whether the user wants to schedule a new meeting with someone named Mark or if they are referring to an existing meeting with a person named Mark.

Pragmatic Ambiguity Resolution.

Understanding the pragmatics of the situation is vital for resolving this ambiguity. The virtual assistant needs to consider the user's likely intention based on the context of the conversation. If there is no previous mention of a meeting with Mark, the pragmatic interpretation would be to schedule a new meeting.

However, if there was a prior conversation about a meeting with Mark, the virtual assistant should interpret the request as modifying or confirming the existing meeting.

Virtual Assistant: "Certainly, I will schedule a new meeting with Mark. What date and time would you prefer?"

By recognizing the pragmatics of the situation, the virtual assistant respond appropriately, either initiating a new task or seeking clarification if there is a potential ambiguity. Pragmatic understanding ensures that the virtual assistant's responses align with the user's intended meaning, providing a more natural and effective interaction.

• • • •

Named Entity Recognition (NER).

• • • •

NLU systems identify and classify named entities in text, such as people's names, locations, dates, and organizations. This is important for information extraction and understanding the content of documents.

Named Entity Recognition (NER) is a fundamental task in NLU where systems identify specific named entities in text. These entities can range from individual names of people to names of organizations, locations, dates, product names, and more. For instance, in the sentence "Joe Biden visited Madrid in 2023 to attend a climate conference,"

NER systems identify "Joe Biden" as a person, "Madrid" as a location, and "2023" as a date.

NER not only recognizes named entities but also classifies them into predefined categories such as persons, organizations, locations, dates, and others. This categorization provides structured information about the entities, enabling further analysis. For example, in the sentence "Apple Inc. is launching its new iPhone in Cupertino next month," NER classifies "Apple Inc." as an organization and "Cupertino" as a location.

NER plays a crucial role in information extraction from unstructured text. By identifying and categorizing entities, NER systems extract relevant information, which will be used for various applications such as creating databases, populating knowledge graphs, and generating structured data from textual sources.

For instance, in a collection of news articles, NER extract names of people, organizations involved, locations, and dates mentioned in the articles, aiding in comprehensive analysis.

In search engines and information retrieval systems, NER enhances the accuracy of searches by understanding specific entities. For instance, when a user searches for "recent books by Noam Chomsky," NER helps identify "Noam Chomsky" as a person and ensures that the search results predominantly include books authored by him, rather than other unrelated content with similar keywords.

NER also encompasses an understanding of entities within their contextual relationships. For instance, in the sentence "Microsoft announced its acquisition of LinkedIn," NER identifies "Microsoft" as an organization and "LinkedIn" as another organization. Understanding this relationship is vital in comprehending complex statements, enabling NLU systems to grasp not just individual entities but also the connections between them.

In legal and compliance fields, NER is crucial for identifying entities mentioned in legal documents. Law firms and regulatory bodies use NER systems to scan contracts, regulations, and other legal texts to identify and categorize entities, ensuring compliance with legal requirements and enabling efficient contract analysis.

NER is language-agnostic, meaning it can be applied to various languages. Multilingual NER is essential in applications like machine translation, cross-lingual information retrieval, and global business intelligence, where understanding entities in multiple languages is crucial for accurate communication and analysis.

Named Entity Recognition is a foundational NLU task that enables systems to identify, classify, and extract specific entities from unstructured text. Its applications are diverse, ranging from information extraction and improving search algorithms to aiding legal analysis and facilitating multilingual communication, making it a pivotal technology in the realm of natural language processing.

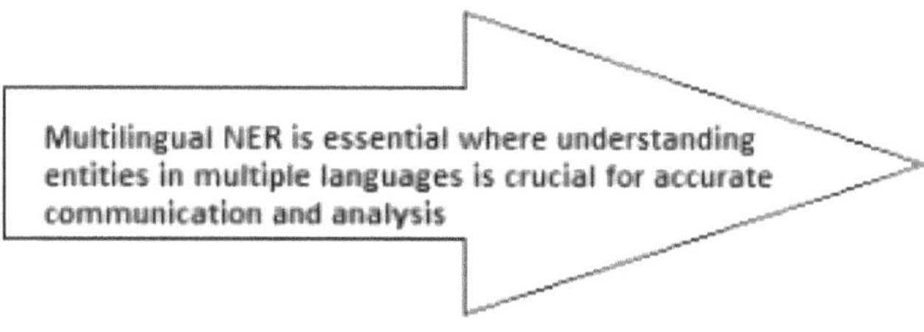

Example: Multilingual Information Retrieval for Business Intelligence.

Scenario: A Global Market Research Firm.

Context: A market research firm is analyzing trends in the smartphone industry across different countries.

Researchers need to retrieve and analyze news articles and reports in multiple languages to understand market dynamics, consumer preferences, and competitor strategies.

Application of Multilingual NER. Data Collection: The research firm collects news articles and reports from various sources in languages like English, Chinese, Spanish, and German. These documents contain valuable information about smartphone companies, product launches, market shares, and consumer feedback.

Multilingual NER algorithms are applied to these documents. For instance, in an English article discussing a new iPhone launch, NER identifies entities like "Apple Inc." (organization), "iPhone 13" (product), and "September 2023" (date). Similarly, in a Chinese article, entities like "[illegible]" (Huawei), "[illegible]" (smartphone), and "[illegible]" (market share) are recognized.

The identified entities are then used for cross-lingual analysis. By comparing entities across different languages, researchers can understand how global smartphone companies are perceived in various markets. For instance, they compare the market presence of "Samsung" in English articles with "[illegible]" (Samsung in Chinese) in Chinese articles, gaining insights into the brand's international reputation.

Multilingual NER collaborates in extracting market trends and consumer sentiment across languages. By identifying and categorizing entities related to consumer feedback, such as "[illegible]" (user reviews) in Chinese articles, researchers can analyze sentiments associated with specific smartphone features and customer experiences in different language markets.

Researchers conduct competitor analysis by comparing mentions of rival companies like "Apple Inc." and "Samsung" in various languages. They identify patterns in how competitors are discussed in different markets and gain insights into regional competitive landscapes.

The application of multilingual NER in this scenario ensures that the research firm to conduct comprehensive cross-lingual analyses. By understanding named entities across languages, researchers uncover valuable insights into international market trends, consumer behavior, and competitive strategies, enabling the firm's clients to make informed decisions in the global smartphone industry.

Example: Multilingual Customer Feedback Analysis for International Brands.

Scenario: Customer Service Analysis for a Global E-commerce Platform.

Context: An international e-commerce platform operates in diverse markets, catering to customers who speak different languages. The company receives customer feedback in various languages, including English, Spanish, French, and German. The platform wants to analyze this feedback to improve customer service and identify common issues faced by customers across different regions.

Application of Multilingual NER:

Customer feedback from product reviews, emails, and social media comments is collected in multiple languages. These texts contain valuable insights into customer experiences, product preferences, and service expectations.

Multilingual NER algorithms are applied to extract entities such as product names, specific features, location names, and organization names from the feedback texts in different languages.

For instance, in English feedback, entities like "iPhone 13," "customer service," and "delivery delay" are identified. In Spanish, entities like "Samsung Galaxy," "servicio al cliente" (customer service), and "retraso en la entrega" (delivery delay) are recognized.

Multilingual NER helps in conducting cross-lingual analysis of customer feedback. By comparing entities across languages, the e-commerce platform identify common issues faced by customers globally. For example, they can discover if a specific product feature, such as "batterie longue durée" (long-lasting battery) in French feedback, is consistently praised or criticized across multiple language markets.

Insights derived from multilingual NER assist the platform in making data-driven decisions. If multiple customers across different languages mention a specific problem with a product, the company prioritize addressing that issue. Likewise, if customers in various regions praise a particular feature, the marketing team can highlight it in their campaigns.

Along with NER, sentiment analysis will be applied to understand the emotional tone of the feedback in different languages. Combining multilingual NER with sentiment analysis enables the platform to identify not only what issues customers are facing but also how these issues are emotionally impacting them across diverse linguistic backgrounds.

The application of multilingual NER in customer feedback analysis enables the e-commerce platform to enhance customer satisfaction globally. By understanding named entities and sentiments in multiple languages, the company tailor its products and services to meet the specific needs of customers in different regions, leading to improved customer experiences and brand loyalty across the international market.

• • • •

Question Answering.

NLU systems are capable of processing questions in natural language and providing relevant answers by extracting information from large datasets or knowledge bases. Question Answering (QA) systems in NLU are designed to comprehend user queries posed in natural language.

These queries range from factual questions like 'What is the capital of Germany?' to more complex questions involving multiple entities and contexts, such as 'What were the main causes of the Industrial Revolution in Europe?'.

To provide accurate answers, QA systems leverage their ability to extract relevant information from vast datasets or knowledge bases. These sources include encyclopedias, textbooks, websites, and other structured and unstructured data repositories. Using techniques like Named Entity Recognition (NER) and semantic analysis, QA systems identify key entities, relationships, and context within the question, enabling targeted information retrieval.

• • • •

QA systems focus on understanding the semantics and context of the question. For example, in the question "When was Marie Curie born?" the system identifies "Marie Curie" as a person and understands that the user is asking for her birth date. Contextual analysis is essential, especially in ambiguous queries. For instance, in the question "What time does the bank open?" understanding the context (banking hours) is necessary to provide a relevant response.

Types of Questions QA Systems Handle:

Fact-Based Questions: QA systems answer straightforward factual questions. For example, 'What is the population of Tokyo?' prompts the system to retrieve the latest population data from a reliable source.

Descriptive Questions: More complex questions require descriptive answers. For instance, 'What are the key principles of quantum physics?' necessitates the system to retrieve comprehensive information and present it in a coherent manner.

Comparative Questions: Users might ask for comparisons like 'Compare iPhone 12 and Samsung Galaxy S21'. QA systems analyze product specifications, user reviews, and expert opinions to provide a detailed comparison.

Procedural Questions: Users seeking step-by-step instructions pose procedural questions. For example, 'How do I bake a chocolate cake?' prompts the system to retrieve a detailed recipe with instructions.

Challenges and Advances:

QA systems face challenges such as understanding complex language nuances, dealing with ambiguous queries, and discerning the most relevant information from extensive datasets. Recent advances in natural language processing, including transformer-based models like GPT-3, have significantly enhanced QA systems' capabilities, allowing them to handle more nuanced queries and provide contextually accurate responses.

QA systems find applications in virtual assistants, customer support chatbots, educational platforms, and information retrieval services. They empower users to obtain specific and reliable information without the need to sift through extensive sources manually, making them invaluable tools in the age of information overload.

Example of a real-world application of Question Answering (QA) systems in customer support chatbots:

Customer Support Chatbot in E-Commerce.

Context: A Customer Seeks Assistance on an E-Commerce Website.

User: "What are the shipping options for my order?"

Application of QA Systems: In this scenario, the user is seeking specific information about shipping options for their order. The e-commerce platform has implemented a QA system within its customer support chatbot.

In this example, the QA system in the customer support chatbot streamlines the interaction, providing tailored information and showcasing the practicality of QA systems in enhancing customer service within the e-commerce industry. The QA system processes the user's query, understanding the semantic meaning and identifying the key entities: "shipping options" and "my order."

The QA system retrieves relevant information from the e-commerce platform's database, accessing details about the user's order and the available shipping options. Based on the retrieved information, the chatbot provides a contextual and accurate response to the user's question:

Chatbot: "Certainly! For your order #[OrderNumber], we offer standard and express shipping options. Standard shipping delivers within 5-7 business days, while express shipping delivers within 2-3 business days. You will choose your preferred option during the checkout process. Is there anything else I can assist you with?'.

The user receives a precise and contextually relevant response to their query about shipping options. The chatbot not only answers the question but also provides additional assistance, creating a seamless and helpful customer experience.

Benefits:

QA systems enable instant responses, enhancing the efficiency of customer support services. Users get quick and accurate answers to their queries.

By providing specific and relevant information, QA-powered chatbots enhance user satisfaction, leading to a positive experience with the e-commerce platform. Customer support agents are freed from handling repetitive queries, freeing them up to concentrate on more complex and specialist problems, improving overall service quality. QA-powered chatbots operate round the clock, ensuring customers can get assistance at any time, even outside regular business hours.

Example: Educational Platform Q&A Feature.

Context: A Student Seeks Help on an Educational Platform.

Student: "Explain the concept of photosynthesis."

In this example, the QA system in the educational platform enriches the student's understanding of the concept of photosynthesis, showcasing the educational benefits of QA systems in online learning environments.

In this scenario, a student on an educational platform is seeking clarification about a scientific concept, photosynthesis. The platform has integrated a QA system to assist students with their queries (Application of QA Systems).

The QA system analyzes the user's query, recognizing the key concept "photosynthesis" and understanding the user's request for an explanation (Semantic Analysis). The QA system accesses the educational platform's database, which includes comprehensive information about various topics, including detailed explanations about photosynthesis (Knowledge Retrieval).

The QA system generates a concise yet informative response (Contextual Response) tailored to the user's query:

QA System: "Photosynthesis is the process by which green plants, algae, and some bacteria convert light energy into chemical energy in the form of glucose. This process occurs in chloroplasts, where chlorophyll, a pigment that captures light energy, is present. During photosynthesis, carbon dioxide and water are used to produce glucose and oxygen. This process is essential for the survival of plants and is the foundation of the food chain. If you have more specific questions or need further details, feel free to ask!"

The student receives a clear and detailed explanation of the concept of photosynthesis. The QA system not only answers the initial question but also encourages the student to ask further questions, promoting a deeper understanding of the topic.

Benefits:

QA systems provide instant, accurate, and detailed explanations, offering valuable educational support to students, especially when they need additional clarification outside the classroom. By encouraging students to ask more questions, QA systems promote personalized learning experiences, empowering students to drill down into topics that interest or challenge them.

QA systems act as supplementary educational tools, reinforcing classroom learning and providing students with access to information in various formats. Educational platforms can handle numerous queries simultaneously, ensuring efficient learning support to a wide range of students, enhancing the overall learning experience.

Example: Travel Assistance Chatbot.

Context: A Traveler Seeks Information on a Travel Website.

Traveler: "What are the must-visit places in Tokyo?"

In this example, the QA system in the travel assistance chatbot enhances the traveler's trip planning experience by providing relevant and engaging recommendations, showcasing the practicality of QA systems in the travel and tourism industry.

In this scenario, a traveler is planning a trip to Tokyo and is looking for recommendations about must-visit places. The travel website has integrated a QA system into its chatbot to assist users with travel-related queries.

The QA system analyzes the user's query, understanding the intent to find notable places in Tokyo that are worth visiting. The QA system accesses its extensive database of travel guides, user reviews, and expert recommendations to retrieve information about popular tourist attractions in Tokyo.

The QA system generates a response tailored to the user's query, offering a list of must-visit places in Tokyo along with brief descriptions:

QA System: "Tokyo offers a plethora of exciting places to explore! Some must-visit places include the historic Senso-ji Temple in Asakusa, the bustling Shibuya Crossing, the iconic Tokyo Tower, the serene Meiji Shrine, and the vibrant districts of Shinjuku and Harajuku.

Additionally, don't miss the teamLab Borderless digital art museum for a unique experience. Each of these places offers a different aspect of Tokyo's rich culture and modern allure. Enjoy your trip!" The traveler receives a personalized list of must-visit places in Tokyo, including diverse attractions that cater to different interests. The QA system's response helps the traveler plan their itinerary effectively.

Benefits:

QA systems provide tailored travel recommendations, assisting users in planning their trips based on their interests and preferences. By combining user reviews and expert recommendations, QA systems offer valuable insights into popular local attractions, enhancing the traveler's experience.

Updates: QA systems can provide up-to-date information, ensuring travelers are aware of any temporary closures, special events, or changes in operating hours for attractions. By offering personalized suggestions, QA systems encourage users to explore further, promoting engagement with the travel platform and enhancing user satisfaction.

. . . .

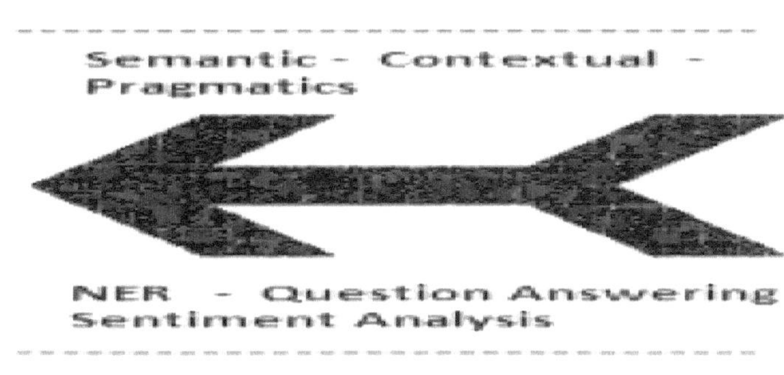

. . . .

Sentiment Analysis.

. . . .

NLU will be utilised to determine the sentiment expressed in a piece of text, such as whether it is positive, egative, or neutral. This is useful for applications like social media monitoring and customer feedback analysis.

Natural Language Understanding (NLU) serves as the gateway to discerning human emotions encoded in textual data. Sentiment analysis, an essential facet of UAL, analyses the feelings contained in words and sentences. Its primary goal is to identify the emotional tone of a piece of text, classifying it as positive, negative, or neutral. By deciphering sentiments, businesses and researchers gain valuable insights into public opinions, enabling informed decision-making

In the digital age, social media platforms are bustling hubs of diverse opinions. Sentiment analysis equips businesses with the ability to gauge public sentiment surrounding their products, services, or even societal events.

By continuously monitoring social media, companies swiftly respond to customer feedback. Positive sentiments are leveraged for marketing campaigns, while negative sentiments prompt proactive damage control strategies. This real-time analysis aids in shaping a positive brand image.

Customer feedback is a goldmine of valuable information. Sentiment analysis acts as a filter, transforming unstructured feedback into structured data. Positive feedback points towards satisfied customers and effective business strategies.

Negative feedback, on the other hand, pinpoints areas needing improvement. Through sentiment analysis, companies identify recurring issues, thus enabling them to enhance their products or services. Moreover, sentiment analysis aids in prioritizing customer complaints, ensuring prompt resolution and customer satisfaction.

Understanding consumer sentiment is a cornerstone of market research. By analyzing textual data from surveys, product reviews, and forums, businesses gain profound insights into market trends. Positive sentiments emphasise the features that resonate with consumers, guiding future product development.

Negative sentiments pinpoint pain points and shortcomings, driving innovation and enhancing customer experience. Market researchers employ sentiment analysis to anticipate market shifts, enabling businesses to stay ahead of the curve. Sentiment analysis extends its reach beyond the corporate realm. In politics, it measures public opinion about policies and political figures, aiding politicians in strategizing their campaigns.

Similarly, in sociological studies, sentiment analysis is employed to analyze public discourse about societal issues. By understanding sentiments, policymakers make informed decisions aligned with public interests, fostering a harmonious society. Sentiment analysis in the context of political and social analysis provide valuable insights into public opinion and societal trends. Let's work with a few examples.

Political Analysis:

Sentiment analysis is applied to social media posts, news articles, and public comments to gauge public sentiment towards political candidates. Positive sentiment might indicate strong support, while negative sentiment could highlight concerns or controversie.

Policymakers use sentiment analysis to understand public reactions to proposed policies. Positive sentiment might suggest that a policy is well-received, while negative sentiment could indicate areas of concern that need to be addressed.

Sentiment analysis is employed to assess public opinion about government initiatives, such as healthcare reforms or environmental policies. This feedback serves policymakers make data-driven decisions and adjust their strategies based on public sentiment.

Social Analysis:

Sentiment analysis analyze social media conversations related to social movements like #BlackLivesMatter or #MeToo. By understanding the sentiment, activists and researchers comprehend public support, identify influential voices, and measure the movement's impact over time.

During health crises like the COVID-19 pandemic, sentiment analysis is used to gauge public reactions to government measures such as lockdowns or vaccination campaigns. Positive sentiment might indicate public cooperation, while negative sentiment could suggest dissatisfaction or confusion, prompting authorities to adjust their communication strategies.

Sentiment analysis track discussions about climate change on social media and news platforms. Positive sentiment might indicate growing awareness and support for environmental initiatives, while negative sentiment could point to skepticism or misinformation that needs to be addressed through education campaigns.

During natural disasters or emergencies, sentiment analysis can monitor social media posts to assess public sentiment. Positive sentiment might indicate resilience and community support, while negative sentiment could highlight areas where aid and resources are urgently needed.

• • • •

Reasoning & Critical Thinking & Make Better Decisions.

Critical thinkers have the ability to objectively and systematically analyze, evaluate, and synthesize information or arguments in order to form well-informed judgments, make reasoned decisions, and solve problems effectively. It implies actively and thoughtfully considering the strengths and weaknesses of ideas, arguments or evidence, rather than accepting them at face value.

Critical thinkers break down complex problems or issues into smaller components to better understand them. They examine the parts, relationships, and connections between various elements. They assess the quality, relevance, and credibility of information, arguments, or solutions. They consider factors like the source's authority, evidence, logic, and potential biases.

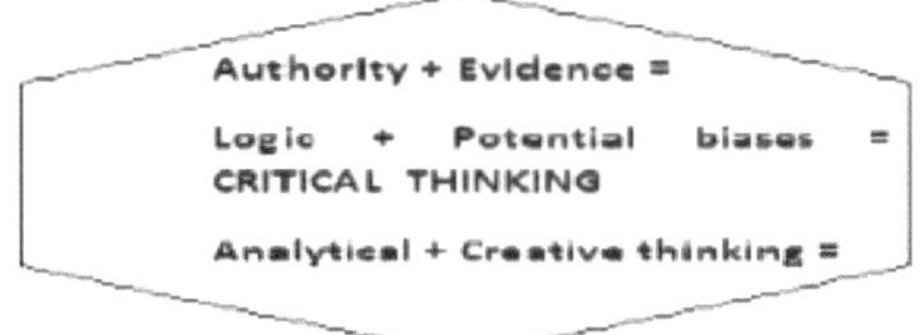

MAKE BETTER DECISIONS
Importance of data Analysis &
Critical Evaluation of Evidence

Critical thinkers draw logical and well-supported conclusions based on available information and evidence. They avoid making unfounded assumptions.

Critical thinking is often applied to problem-solving. It involves identifying problems or challenges, generating and evaluating potential solutions, and selecting the most appropriate course of action. While critical thinking is analytical, it also allows for creative thinking when seeking innovative solutions or considering alternative perspectives.

Critical thinkers are open to different viewpoints and willing to consider ideas that may challenge their existing beliefs or assumptions. They approach issues with intellectual humility. They express their ideas and reasoning clearly and persuasively.

Empowering individuals to think more critically and make better decisions requires a combination of education, practice, and the cultivation of certain habits and skills. Strategies to help individuals develop and strengthen their critical thinking and decision-making abilities:

Encourage individuals to seek a broad education that exposes them to diverse topics and perspectives. Instruct in techniques of information literacy, such as evaluating sources, detecting bias and verifying sources.

Support lifelong learning by exploring new topics, reading widely, and seeking out new experiences. Teach problem-solving techniques and strategies for breaking down complex issues into manageable parts.

Underline the significance of data analysis and critical evaluation of evidence.

Promote empathy and encourage people to consider different points of view and experiences. To promote empathy and inspire people to consider different points of view and experiences. Foster self-reflection and self-awareness. Individuals should periodically evaluate their thought processes and decision-making patterns.

Encourage open and respectful dialogue in which people engage in discussion, debate and exchange of ideas. To promote active listening and constructive feedback. Focus on critical reading through the analysis of texts, articles and books. Develop persuasive writing, argumentation and clear communication of ideas.

AI-powered information retrieval systems and chatbots provide individuals with access to accurate and reliable information on a wide range of topics. This combat misinformation and fosters informed discussions, leading to greater cohesion.

Artificial Intelligence (AI) contribute to social cohesion in various ways by addressing challenges, fostering inclusivity, and promoting understanding among individuals and communities.

AI offers cultural sensitivity training and resources to individuals and organizations, them navigate diverse cultural contexts with respect and understanding. AI facilitate the creation of online communities where people with shared interests or backgrounds connect and build relationships. These communities promote a sense of belonging and cohesion.

AI analyze vast amounts of data to identify social issues and disparities, such as inequalities in education, healthcare, or employment. This data-driven insight inform policies and interventions to promote social cohesion.

AI-powered personalized learning platforms adapt educational content to individual learners, catering to their needs and abilities. This bridge educational gaps and promote equal opportunities. AI-driven telemedicine and diagnostic tools improve access to healthcare, particularly in underserved areas, contributing to better overall community health and cohesion.

AI assists in designing products and environments with accessibility and inclusivity in mind, ensuring that people with disabilities participate fully in society. AI help law enforcement agencies identify areas with a high risk of crime, enabling more targeted and proactive policing to enhance community safety.

AI optimizes resource allocation and support initiatives related to environmental sustainability, which lead to improved living conditions and social cohesion. AI assist in optimizing the allocation of social services, such as welfare programs and housing, ensuring that those in need receive appropriate support.

AI aids in disaster response efforts by analyzing data to identify affected areas and mobilize resources efficiently, strengthening community resilience. AI contribute to the preservation of endangered languages by assisting in transcription, translation, and documentation efforts. We will elaborate on these issues further along.

It's important to note that while AI offer many benefits for social cohesion, there are also ethical considerations, including concerns about bias in AI algorithms, data privacy, and the responsible use of technology. Careful design, transparency, and ongoing evaluation of AI systems are essential to ensure that they contribute positively to social cohesion without reinforcing inequalities or biases.

• • • •

What about the veracity of the messages received through this channel, how can we be sure that the data provided is true?.

Verifying the veracity of information received through any communication channel, including digital ones like this, is essential in today's age of information. No verification process is foolproof, and misinformation can still sometimes spread. It's essential to be vigilant and use a combination of critical thinking and reliable sources to make informed judgments about the veracity of the information we encounter.

Verify the credibility of the source providing the information. Is it a reputable organization or individual with expertise in the relevant field?. We must be cautious of sources that are not well-established or known to disseminate accurate information.

Try to cross-reference the information receive with multiple reliable sources. If the same information is reported by multiple reputable sources, it's more likely to be accurate.

Apply critical thinking skills to the information. Consider whether it aligns with the existing knowledge and whether it seems logical and plausible. Be skeptical of claims that seem too good to be true or overly sensational.

Use fact-checking websites and tools to verify specific claims or statements. Fact-checkers independently assess the accuracy of claims made in news articles, social media posts, and other sources.

In academic or technical contexts, peer-reviewed publications are a valuable source of reliable information. Look for research papers and articles that have been reviewed by experts in the field. Consider the context in which the information is presented. Sometimes, information can be accurate but taken out of context, leading to a misunderstanding.

We must be cautious when dealing with anonymous sources or messages. While anonymity will be necessary in some cases, it also makes it more challenging to verify the credibility of the information.

If we are receiving information through a specific platform or channel, such as a website, social media, or email, we should ensure that the platform itself is secure and has measures in place to combat misinformation.

Engage in discussions with others who have knowledge in the area in question. Public forums, academic communities, and social media provide opportunities for collaborative fact-checking and information verification.

If the information is critical or highly specialized, we should consider seeking the opinion of experts in the field, they provide insights and context that help to assess the accuracy of the information. Recognize that bias exist in information sources. Understand the potential biases of the sources to consult and consider how those biases might affect the information being presented.

1.2. The Fusion of Linguistic and Mathematical Approaches

What we do know is that words become vectors and two worlds come together: the linguistic and the mathematical.

We think that artificial intelligence is very intelligent because it thinks, but it doesn't really think, it's just a mathematical formulation of something you ask it to do (see GPT chat def). What it is actually doing is predicting something that has already happened, that we have fed it and trained it, and that is how it is able to process all the data.

The AI works on a mathematical decision table and answers A or B based on certain criteria. The two big nuances are that, on the one hand, it does not have freedom, will and reason, which is what distinguishes the individual from the machine. And the second nuance is that it cannot get inside people's heads and hearts, it cannot know what only you know about yourself.

Are we far superior to machines?. Or are they superior to us?. The idea of a superior being is only good for science fiction films. That is, if we unplug the machine, this superior entity disappears. People are slower in areas such as arithmetic or reading, but we do many other things that the new technological models, despite their enormous capabilities, cannot do, such as the ability to reason (I wonder if Noam Chomsky would agree).

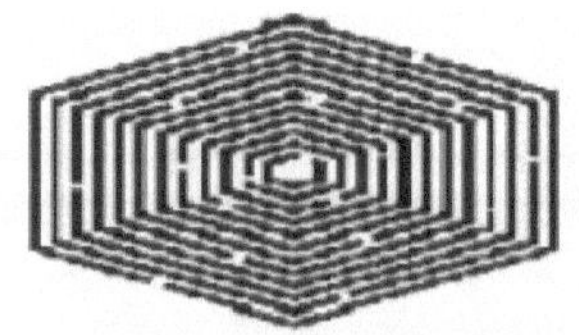

Confluence of the linguistic and mathematical domains

The fusion of linguistic and mathematical approaches in NLU combines the strengths of both disciplines. Linguistic insights provide a foundation for understanding the subtleties of human language, while mathematical modeling offers the computational power to process and analyze large volumes of text data efficiently.

As AI systems aim to converse with people more naturally, comprehend context, and generate coherent text, this interdisciplinary collaboration is becoming increasingly vital. Linguistics provides the foundational understanding of language's intricacies, while mathematics equips AI with the tools to process and analyze language data at scale.

By melding these approaches, we are poised to develop AI systems that can truly understand, interpret, and generate human language effectively, opening the door to a wide range of applications, from chatbots and virtual assistants to advanced language translation and sentiment analysis.

On the other hand, the Fusion of Linguistic and Mathematical Approaches represents a Catalyst for Interdisciplinary Research in Artificial Intelligence. The complexity and depth of AI challenges often require a fusion of expertise from diverse domains. The integration of linguistic and mathematical approaches is poised to not only enhance but also revolutionize interdisciplinary research in the context of AI.

Linguistics, leaves no stone unturned, exploring the structural, semantic, and pragmatic aspects of language. In doing so, it sheds light on the intricate ways in which words and sentences convey meaning and context. This profound understanding of language is a foundational pillar for AI, as it equips machines with the ability to bridge the gap between people language and computational logic.

Linguistic analysis in AI is not merely about recognizing words; it's about understanding the structure, semantics, and pragmatics of people language. These linguistic insights are the building blocks for AI's ability to decode and interpret people communication effectively.

By enabling machines to comprehend context, meaning, and nuance, linguistic analysis empowers AI systems to provide more accurate responses, make informed decisions, and engage in more natural and meaningful interactions with users.

Mathematics, renowned for its precision and logical rigor, provides a powerful framework for modeling complex phenomena. In the realm of AI, mathematical modeling is not just an auxiliary tool but a fundamental cornerstone that underpins a wide array of applications and research endeavors.

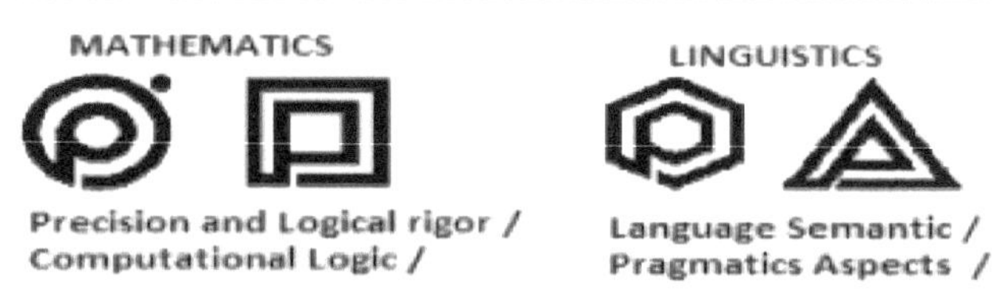

One of the primary domains where mathematical modeling shines in AI is machine learning. Machine learning algorithms are designed to learn from data, and mathematical models provide the formalism to represent and manipulate this data effectively.

Through mathematical frameworks like linear algebra, calculus, and probability theory, machine learning models can grasp intricate patterns and relationships within datasets. For instance, in image recognition, mathematical models discern intricate features and shapes in images, thereby permitting AI systems to recognise objects and scenes accurately.

Moreover, data analysis in AI heavily relies on mathematical techniques. Whether it's exploratory data analysis, data preprocessing, or statistical inference, mathematics enables AI researchers to make sense of vast and complex datasets. Mathematical statistics, for example, provides the tools to draw meaningful conclusions from data, then AI practitioners extract valuable insights, identify trends, and make data-driven decisions.

Algorithm development, a fundamental component of AI research, also leans on mathematical foundations. Developing efficient algorithms often requires a deep understanding of computational complexity theory, optimization, and graph theory, all of which are branches of mathematics.

Mathematical algorithms not only optimize the performance of AI systems but also enable the development of novel approaches to complex problems. For instance, mathematical optimization techniques are employed in training deep neural networks to achieve state-of-the-art performance in various tasks, from image recognition to natural language processing.

In addition to these core areas, mathematical approaches offer the advantage of handling large datasets, a ubiquitous challenge in AI research. Through techniques like matrix factorization and parallel processing, mathematicians and AI researchers collaborate to develop efficient algorithms that process and analyze vast volumes of data.

This capability is vital in applications such as recommendation systems, where mathematical models sift through extensive user behavior data to provide personalized recommendations. The example of 'life2vec', this system, is also able to predict aspects of people's personalities, such as their level of sociability and is able to predict a person's death for the next four years of their life.

Furthermore, mathematical models excel in making predictions, a critical aspect of AI research. Whether it's predicting future trends in financial markets, forecasting weather patterns, or estimating the likelihood of a medical diagnosis, mathematical modeling empowers

AI to provide invaluable insights and foresight. In financial markets, for instance, advanced mathematical models employ historical data and statistical methods to anticipate market fluctuations, helping investors make informed decisions and mitigate risks. In meteorology, mathematical models simulate the behavior of the Earth's atmosphere, enabling meteorologists to make accurate weather predictions, plan for severe weather events, and issue timely warnings to protect lives and property.

In interdisciplinary research within AI, the fusion of linguistic and mathematical approaches leverages these predictive capabilities to unlock new dimensions. For instance, linguistic data combined with mathematical models predict sentiment trends in social media, aiding in understanding public opinion or consumer preferences.

Linguistic and mathematical sinergy

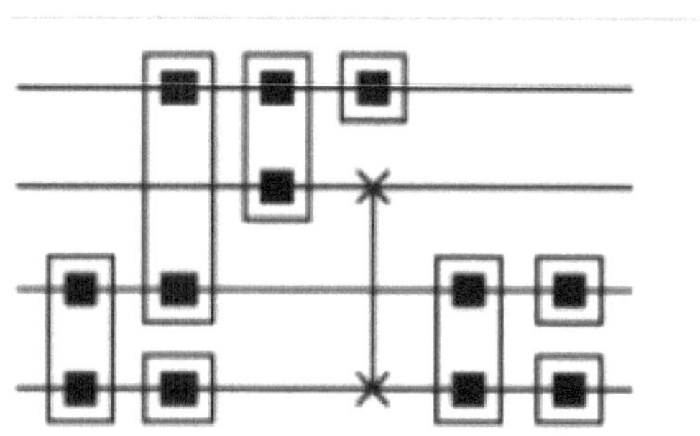

Mathematical modeling in AI is not merely a tool but a driving force that empowers AI systems to make informed decisions, anticipate future events, and optimize processes. The fusion of linguistic and mathematical approaches within interdisciplinary research expands the horizons of what AI achieve, offering new innovative solutions to complex problems in diverse domains.

Whether it's enhancing natural language understanding, advancing medical research, or revolutionizing financial forecasting, the synergy between linguistic and mathematical approaches in AI research opens doors to a future of unprecedented possibilities.

Rather than just predicting or making decisions, AI solutions should be developed to conduct exploratory analyses, i.e., to find new, interesting patterns in complex systems or facilitate scientific discovery

While AI algorithms still focus mainly on modelling purely cognitive processes (e.g. learning, abstraction, planning...), a complementary approach could regard intelligence as an emergent property of cognitive systems through their coupling with environmental, morphological, sensorimotor, developmental, social, cultural and evolutionary processes.

Of course, combining AI with other fields is not without its difficulties. As always when there is synergy between fields, there are communication barriers due to differences in terminology, methodology, culture and interests. How to bridge these gaps remains an open question, but a solid background in both machine learning and the field of interest is clearly a must.

To explore this need, we discuss here three key challenges for interdisciplinary AI research, and draw three general findings:

* The future development of AI should not only have an impact on other scientific fields, but should also draw upon and benefit from other fields of science,

* AI research should be accompanied by the explicitness of decisions, transparency of biases in datasets, as well as the further development of evaluation methodologies and the creation of regulatory bodies to ensure accountability, and

* AI education should receive more attention, effort and innovation from the educational and scientific communities.

Is AI working on the basis of a Mathematical Decision Table?.

• • • •

That statement is not accurate. Artificial Intelligence does not operate on the basis of a table of mathematical decisions. AI has a wide range of techniques and approaches, and its functionality is not limited to a single mathematical concept or model.

AI is a diverse field that spans a wide range of mathematical and computational approaches, and is not limited to a single "mathematical decision table". AI researchers and practitioners select and develop the most appropriate mathematical and computational methods for the particular tasks and problems they intend to solve.

AI, or artificial intelligence, concerns the development of computer systems and algorithms that perform tasks that normally require human intelligence. These range from problem solving, pattern recognition, natural language understanding and decision making.

AI techniques are classified into several subfields, such as machine learning, deep learning, natural language processing, computer vision and expert systems, amongst many others.

While mathematical concepts, algorithms and models are certainly integral to many AI approaches, they are not limited to a single decision table. AI models are based on mathematical principles such as linear algebra, calculus, probability theory and statistical modelling.

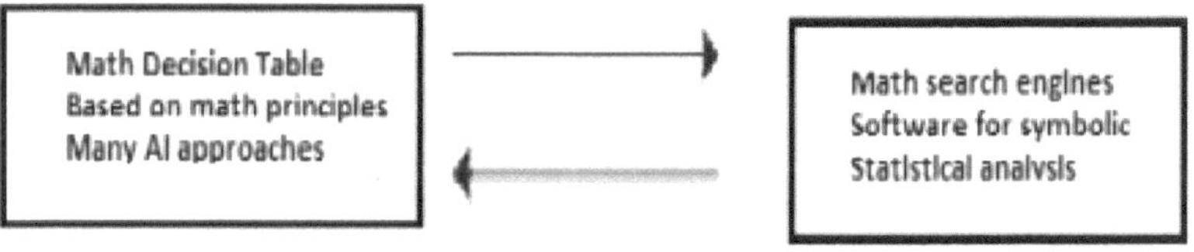

Machine learning, for example, involves training models on data to make predictions or decisions, but the underlying mathematical structures may vary greatly depending on the specific AI technique used.

Machine learning, for example, empowers AI systems to learn and adapt from data, enhancing their performance over time. Deep learning, a subset of machine learning, involves neural networks capable of intricate learning patterns. Natural language processing enables machines to comprehend and interact with human language, while computer vision imparts the ability to interpret and analyze visual information.

For its side, 'mathematical search engines' has the ability to search for specific mathematical formulas, equations, theorems, and mathematical expressions. Users input mathematical notation or keywords related to their mathematical query.

These search engines are tailored to the specific needs of mathematicians, students, researchers, educators, and anyone seeking mathematical content. Mathematical search engines leverage algorithms and mathematical databases to deliver relevant and accurate results to users' mathematical queries.

Users search for explanations and definitions of mathematical concepts and terms. Mathematical search engines often provide access to a wide range of mathematical problems and their solutions. Users search for solutions to specific math problems or browse through collections of math exercises and solutions for educational purposes.

These search engines strengthens researchers and academics find scholarly articles, research papers, and publications related to their mathematical fields of interest. Users search for academic content on specific topics or authors.

Mathematical search engines may also guide users discover mathematical software, tools, and resources for performing calculations, simulations, and data analysis. This comprises software for symbolic math, graphing, statistical analysis, and more. Moreover, grant teachers and students access to educational materials, including textbooks, online courses, lecture notes, and tutorials.

Some mathematical search engines may connect users with online communities and forums where they ask questions, discuss mathematical topics, and collaborate with other mathematicians, they will search for specific mathematical symbols, notations, and conventions.

• • • •

Mathematics Assistance & Bridging Language Barriers.

It encompasses the use of IA for the use of artificial intelligence (AI) and natural language processing (NLP) technologies to provide support, guidance, and help with mathematical tasks and problems.

On the other hand, mathematics assistance tutoring users solve mathematical problems of varying complexity. This include basic arithmetic, algebra, calculus, geometry, and more. Users input math problems in natural language, and the system provide step-by-step solutions or explanations.

AI-powered mathematics assistance act as a virtual math tutor, helping students understand mathematical concepts and principles. It provide explanations, examples, and practice problems tailored to a user's skill level and learning pace.

Some mathematics assistance tools are capable of symbolic math manipulation. They perform algebraic simplifications, solve equations, differentiate and integrate functions, and work with mathematical symbols and expressions. Mathematics assistance tools generate graphs and visual representations of mathematical concepts. For example, they plot functions, illustrate geometric shapes, and show the graphical solutions to equations.

Wolfram Alpha, SymPy, Microsoft Math Solver, SymbMath, Desmos, are powerful AI tools that performs symbolic mathematics. It enables users to evaluate, simplify, and solve algebraic expressions and equations, to enhance mathematical visualization and exploration, simplifying formulas, and performing symbolic computations.

These access vast mathematical knowledge bases to provide information on mathematical concepts, theorems, and formulas. Users inquire about specific mathematical topics or properties. Users ask natural language questions related to mathematics, and the system provide concise and accurate answers.

Mathematics assistance assist students with their homework and assignments by guiding them through problems, checking their work, and offering suggestions for improvement. In addition to academic math, mathematics assistance have applications in various real-world scenarios, such as engineering, finance, data analysis, and scientific research.

Through the bridging Language Barriers, artificial intelligence (AI) and natural language processing (NLP) technologies overcome the challenges posed by language differences and facilitate communication between people who speak different languages.

Overall, the goal of bridging language barriers with AI is to promote understanding, communication, and collaboration among people and cultures that speak different languages. These technologies are essential for our increasingly interconnected and globalized world, where effective communication across language boundaries is crucial for personal, business, and societal interactions.

One of the primary ways AI contributes to bridging language barriers is through translation services. AI-powered translation tools automatically convert text or spoken words from one language into another. This is incredibly useful for travelers, businesses, and individuals who need to communicate with people from different language backgrounds.

Some AI systems provide real-time or instant translation during spoken conversations. This enables people who don't share a common language to communicate effectively by speaking in their native languages, with the AI system translating their words for each party.

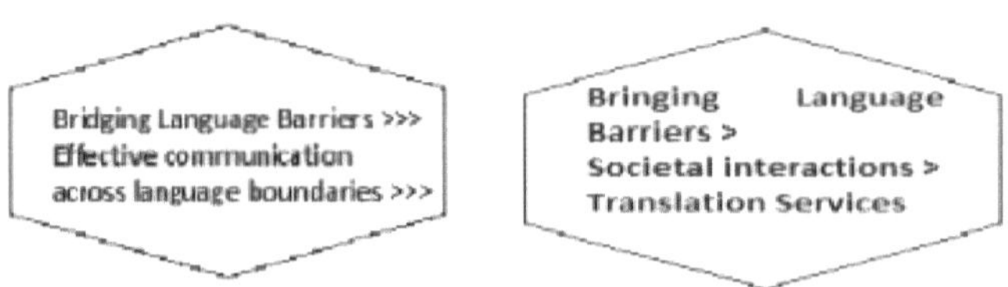

AI enable users to access information and content in languages they may not understand. For example, AI translate web pages, documents, or social media posts into the user's preferred language, making information more accessible globally.

AI-powered language learning platforms assist individuals in acquiring new languages. These systems often offer interactive lessons, pronunciation correction, and personalized language exercises to help users become proficient in a foreign language.

Businesses use AI chatbots and virtual assistants to provide customer support in multiple languages. This ensures that customers from diverse linguistic backgrounds receive assistance and information in their preferred language.

AI systems designed to bridge language barriers also consider cultural nuances and differences. This helps avoid misunderstandings and misinterpretations, which is particularly important in cross-cultural communication. Can make content more accessible for individuals with language-related disabilities. For example, it provide text-to-speech or speech-to-text services for people who are deaf or hard of hearing.

• • • •

'Analogical Reasoning' in the AI context.

• • • •

Analogical reasoning in the context of artificial intelligence (AI) envelopes us in that complex world where ability of AI systems to recognize and apply analogies or similarities between different situations, domains, or concepts. It involves finding relationships, patterns, and similarities between entities or ideas and using these relationships to draw inferences, make predictions, or solve problems.

An analogy is a comparison between two or more entities or situations that underline their similarities in certain respects while ignoring differences. It is often expressed in the form "A is to B as C is to D," where A, B, C, and D are entities or concepts.—-Definition of Analogy:

AR is a key aspect of people cognition and intelligence. It enables people to learn from past experiences, solve novel problems, and make connections between seemingly unrelated ideas. In AI, replicating this ability is crucial for creative problem-solving and knowledge transfer.

One classic example of analogical reasoning is the analogy between "the human heart is to the circulatory system as the engine is to a car." This analogy highlights the role of the heart in pumping blood through the circulatory system, similar to how the engine powers a car.

Analogical reasoning is often used in natural language processing (NLP) tasks. For instance, word embeddings and vector representations of words can capture semantic relationships and analogies. For example, the relationship between "king" and "queen" can be represented as an analogy: "king - queen ≈ man - woman."

Analogical reasoning is closely related to common sense reasoning, as it involves applying general knowledge and principles to new situations. Common sense knowledge often includes analogies and metaphors that help in understanding and reasoning about the world.

AI systems use analogical reasoning in various ways, such as in case-based reasoning, where past cases are used to solve new problems by finding analogies between cases. AI also use analogies for transfer learning, where knowledge learned in one domain is applied to another domain.

Analogical reasoning (AR) remains a challenging problem in AI because it requires identifying relevant similarities and transferring knowledge effectively. Building AI systems that perform analogical reasoning at a human-like level is an ongoing research area. AR has applications in recommendation systems, knowledge representation and reasoning, creative problem-solving, scientific discovery, and education, among others.

Some AI models and systems use analogy-based learning to acquire new knowledge by recognizing analogies between known facts and new information. Efforts to advance analogical reasoning in AI aim to improve the ability of AI systems to generalize knowledge, adapt to new situations, and engage in more creative problem-solving.

Analogical reasoning stands as a cornerstone of people intelligence, offering the individuals to bridge the gap between familiar and unfamiliar situations, drawing upon prior experiences to understand new concepts.

Analogies serve as mental bridges, so that people will be able to recall and apply lessons learned from previous experiences to current situations. By recognizing similarities between past scenarios and present challenges, humans can adapt strategies that have proven successful in the past.

When confronted with new and unfamiliar problems, humans often rely on analogies. By recognizing analogous patterns between the current problem and something they've encountered before, individuals apply previously successful solutions to novel situations, fostering innovative problem-solving.

AR aids in making connections between disparate fields of knowledge. It encourages interdisciplinary thinking, permitting individuals to transfer concepts and solutions from one domain to another. This interdisciplinary approach is vital for innovation, as breakthroughs often occur at the intersection of different fields.

AR is crucial for AI systems engaged in creative tasks. Whether composing music, generating art, or designing novel solutions, AI that draw analogies between diverse artistic or problem-solving contexts produce innovative and creative outcomes.

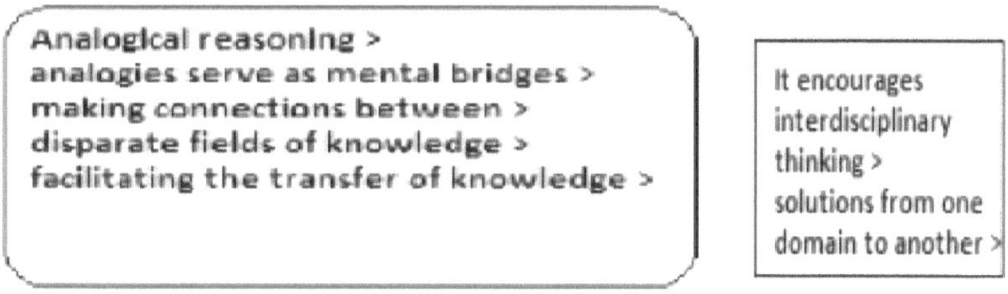

AR in AI facilitates the transfer of knowledge from one domain to another. Just as humans apply knowledge from one area to solve problems in another, AI systems utilize analogies to transfer learned patterns and solutions, enhancing their adaptability across various applications.

Analogical reasoning is foundational to transfer learning in AI, this enables AI models to leverage knowledge gained from one task to improve performance on another related task. By recognizing analogies between tasks, AI systems generalize learning, enhancing their efficiency and accuracy in diverse applications.

AI systems equipped with analogical reasoning capabilities innovate in problem-solving scenarios. By recognizing analogous problems and solutions, these systems propose unconventional yet effective approaches, fostering breakthroughs in various fields such as scientific research, engineering, and healthcare.

· · · ·

Analogical Reasoning in Natural Language Processing (NLP): Semantic Relationships.

· · · ·

In natural language processing (NLP), analogical reasoning is a powerful mechanism that would let AI systems to discern semantic relationships between words and concepts. This capability is vital for several reasons.

In NLP, words are often represented as high-dimensional vectors in a continuous vector space, known as word embeddings. These embeddings are learned from vast amounts of text data using techniques like Word2Vec, GloVe, or FastText. Analogical reasoning is implicit in these embeddings. For instance, in a well-trained word embedding space, the vector difference between words capture relationships.

The fundamental premise of Word2Vec is that words with similar meanings tend to co-occur in similar contexts. In other words, words that frequently appear together in sentences tend to be connected in meaning. Word2Vec takes advantage of this idea to generate vector depictions of words based on their co-occurrence patterns in a large corpus of text.

Through the analogical reasoning AI systems might be able to capture and understand various semantic relationships between words. For example, by recognizing the relationship "king is to queen as man is to woman," AI models learn to represent these relationships in vector space. In the embedding space, the vector difference between "king" and "queen" is approximately equal to the vector difference between "man" and "woman."

AR enables the discovery of semantic analogies. In the example above, if a system understands the analogy, it answer queries like 'What is to woman as king is to man?.' The AI model, by performing vector arithmetic, would find that the answer is 'queen.'

It's essential to note that word embeddings inadvertently capture cultural and social biases present in the training data. Analogies inferred from these embeddings might reflect these biases, which has raised ethical concerns in the field of AI. Researchers are actively working to mitigate these biases to ensure fair and unbiased language processing.

AR enhances various NLP tasks. For instance, in machine translation, understanding semantic analogies helps in translating idiomatic expressions and phrases that don't have direct word-toword translations. In question-answering systems, recognizing analogies aids in understanding implicit relationships in questions and passages.

While traditional word embeddings provide static representations of words, recent advancements such as contextual word embeddings (e.g., ELMo, BERT, GPT) offer dynamic word representations that consider the context of the surrounding words. These contextual embeddings improve the understanding of word meanings in different contexts, enabling more nuanced analogical reasoning.

• • • •

BERT	GPT
Bidirectional. Can process text left-to-right and right-to-left. BERT uses the encoder segment of a transformation model.	Autoregressive and unidirectional. Text is processed in one direction. GPT uses the decoder segment of a transformation model.
Applied in Google Docs, Gmail, smart compose, enhanced search, voice assistance, analyzing customer reviews, and so on.	Applied in application building, generating ML code, websites, writing articles, podcasts, creating legal documents, and so on.
GLUE score = 80.4% and 93.3% accuracy on the SQUAD dataset.	64.3% accuracy on the TriviaAQ benchmark and 76.2% accuracy on LAMBADA, with zero-shot learning
Uses two unsupervised tasks, masked language modeling, fill in the blanks and next sentence prediction e.g. does sentence B come after sentence A?	Straightforward text generation using autoregressive language modeling.

• • • •

Analogical Reasoning & Common Sense Reasoning.

• • • •

Common sense reasoning involves applying general knowledge, intuitions, and everyday experiences to make sense of new situations. Analogical reasoning, on the other hand, draws individuals to similar past experiences and apply them to novel contexts. Analogies, serving as bridges between familiar and unfamiliar situations, are a common thread between the two processes.

Common sense knowledge often comprises everyday analogies and metaphors that simplify complex concepts. These linguistic constructs are based on analogical reasoning, enabling individuals to explain abstract or unfamiliar ideas in terms of more accessible, familiar concepts.

For instance, explaining the concept of electricity as "flowing like water" is an analogy that aids in common understanding.

Analogical reasoning, driven by the recognition of similarities between situations, gives individuals the opportunity to transfer solutions from known problems to unfamiliar ones. Common sense reasoning guides this process by providing general principles and knowledge about how the world works. By recognizing analogous patterns, individuals can navigate new challenges effectively.

Both analogical and common sense reasoning contribute to contextual understanding. Analogies often rely on shared contextual knowledge. Common sense reasoning enables individuals to grasp the implicit context of a situation, enhancing the recognition and creation of analogies.

Analogical reasoning serves as a fundamental mechanism for learning from analogies present in everyday language and experiences. Common sense reasoning guides the interpretation of these analogies, offering the option for individuals to extract meaningful lessons and principles from diverse situations.

In artificial intelligence, the ability to understand and generate analogies is a significant challenge. Analogies are prevalent in human communication and are deeply embedded in common sense knowledge. AI systems that comprehend these analogies and relate them to common sense principles achieve a more profound level of natural language understanding.

AR often involves making connections between different domains of knowledge. Common sense reasoning enables individuals to recognize these cross-domain connections, facilitating creative thinking and problem-solving. In AI, models capable of crossdomain analogical reasoning generate innovative solutions in diverse fields.

• • • •

Analogical Reasoning in Scientific Discovery.

• • • •

Scientists frequently encounter situations where existing theories are insufficient to explain a new phenomenon. Analogical reasoning identifies patterns and similarities between the new and known phenomena in different domains. By recognizing these analogies, scientists gain new perspectives and formulate hypotheses to explain the unexplained.

Analogies serve as a foundation for formulating hypotheses. When scientists recognize an analogy between a well-understood phenomenon and a puzzling new observation, they can hypothesize that similar principles might apply. These hypotheses guide further experimentation and investigation, leading to a deeper understanding of the new phenomenon.

Analogical reasoning sparks creativity in scientific problem-solving. By drawing analogies from diverse fields, scientists devise innovative experimental approaches and methodologies. Creative solutions often arise from adapting techniques or concepts from one domain to address challenges in another, leading to breakthroughs in scientific research.

AR encourages interdisciplinary research. When scientists identify analogies between phenomena in different scientific disciplines, it motivates collaboration between researchers from diverse fields. This collaboration fosters the exchange of knowledge and methodologies, leading to holistic and innovative approaches to scientific problems.

Throughout the history of science, analogical reasoning has played a pivotal role in major discoveries. For instance, James Clerk Maxwell's use of analogies between electrical and mechanical systems led to the formulation of Maxwell's equations, which describe electromagnetic phenomena. Albert Einstein's theory of relativity was inspired by analogies drawn between acceleration and gravity, fundamentally transforming our understanding of space and time.

$$\oint \vec{E} \cdot d\vec{A} = \frac{q}{\varepsilon_0}$$

$$\oint \vec{B} \cdot d\vec{A} = 0$$

Symbols Used		
E = Electric field	ρ = charge density	i = electric current
B = Magnetic field	ε_0 = permittivity	J = current density
D = Electric displacement	μ_0 = permeability	c = speed of light
H = Magnetic field strength	M = Magnetization	P = Polarization

Source: hyperphysics

Scientists often create analogical models to represent complex or abstract theories. These models use familiar concepts to illustrate intricate scientific principles. Analogical reasoning guides the creation of these models, making scientific theories more accessible to both scientists and the general public.

In areas of scientific exploration where little is known, analogical reasoning becomes a guiding principle. By drawing analogies from established fields, scientists formulate hypotheses and design experiments to explore uncharted territories, paving the way for new scientific discoveries.

In the realm of artificial intelligence, machine learning algorithms are increasingly being used to discover analogies within vast datasets. These algorithms identify patterns and relationships, potentially leading to novel scientific hypotheses. AI-driven analogical reasoning accelerates the pace of scientific discovery by guiding scientists toward promising areas of research.

Artificial Intelligence (AI) systems draws also on analogical reasoning, particularly in case-based reasoning and transfer learning, to solve complex problems and enhance their learning capabilities.

From solving practical problems through case-based reasoning to enhancing learning and creativity through transfer learning and metaphorical reasoning, analogical reasoning empowers AI systems to learn, reason, and create in ways that parallel human cognitive processes.

CBR is a problem-solving paradigm in AI where past experiences, or cases, are stored and reused to solve new, similar problems. Analogical reasoning forms the core of CBR. When faced with a new problem, the AI system identifies analogous situations from the stored cases.

By recognizing similarities in the problem structure and context, the system adapts solutions from past cases to address the new problem. CBR finds applications in diverse domains such as medical diagnosis, troubleshooting, and legal reasoning, where solutions from analogous cases are invaluable.

Transfer learning is a machine learning technique where knowledge gained from one domain is applied to improve learning or performance in another related domain. Analogical reasoning enables AI models to recognize similarities between the source domain (where the model is trained) and the target domain (where the model needs to perform).

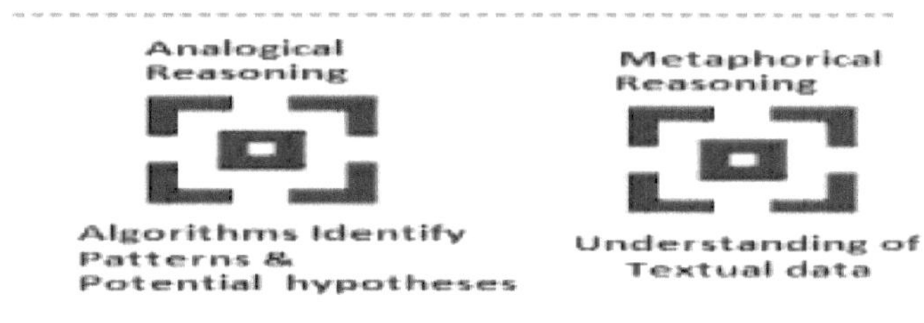

How scientists utilize analogies to formulate hypotheses and develop new theories. Scientific discovery is a multifaceted process that often relies on analogical reasoning, enabling scientists to make connections between seemingly disparate phenomena and generate innovative insights.

By drawing analogies between these domains, AI systems transfer relevant knowledge, features, or representations from the source to the target domain. This process enhances the efficiency of learning in the target domain, particularly when data is limited or expensive to acquire.

Metaphorical reasoning involves understanding metaphors and analogies in human language. AI systems analyze metaphors to grasp deeper meanings in text. For instance, understanding phrases like "time is money" involves recognizing the metaphorical analogy between time and money. Metaphor-based reasoning enriches AI's comprehension of people language, enabling more nuanced understanding of textual data.

In computer vision, analogical reasoning is applied to visual data. AI systems recognize visual analogies, where similarities between images or scenes are identified. For example, in image recognition, recognizing that two images share analogous objects or structures contributes in classifying or understanding the content of the images. Visual analogies are valuable in tasks like image captioning, object recognition, and scene understanding.

Analogical reasoning in AI extends to creative domains. AI-driven creative systems, such as those generating art or music, use analogies to blend styles or generate innovative compositions. By drawing analogies between different artistic styles or musical genres, AI systems create novel and aesthetically pleasing outputs, showcasing the creativity of machines.

AI systems analyze vast datasets in scientific research. Analogical reasoning contributes to identify patterns and similarities between different scientific phenomena. Scientists use AI to propose hypotheses based on these analogies, leading to new experiments and discoveries.

> Analogical reasoning poses several intricate challenges in the realm of artificial intelligence, reflecting the complexities of human-like cognitive processes.

> Analogies often rely on context >
> Ambiguity in language >
> Contextual understanding techniques >

· · · ·

One of the primary challenges lies in identifying pertinent similarities between situations or concepts. Human minds excel at intuitively recognizing subtle connections, but teaching AI systems to discern these nuanced similarities requires sophisticated algorithms. Relevant features must be identified and compared across diverse contexts, demanding advanced pattern recognition capabilities.

Analogies often rely on context, and understanding the context of a situation is vital for accurate analogical reasoning. Ambiguity in language, situations, or data further complicates this process. AI systems must navigate this ambiguity and contextual variance to draw accurate analogies, necessitating contextual understanding techniques that adapt to different scenarios.

Analogical reasoning (AR) requires a robust representation of knowledge. AI systems need structured and semantically rich knowledge bases to draw meaningful analogies. Representing knowledge in a format suitable for analogical reasoning, where relationships between entities are well-defined and accessible, is a challenge.

Knowledge graphs and ontologies are common approaches used to represent knowledge, but refining these structures for nuanced analogical reasoning remains an active research area.

In real-world applications, AI systems encounter vast and diverse datasets. Effective analogical reasoning demands the ability to sift through this enormous data landscape to find relevant analogies. Handling diverse data formats, languages, and sources requires AI systems to generalize analogical reasoning techniques, ensuring applicability across varied contexts.

AR often reflects societal and cultural biases present in the training data. AI systems might unintentionally perpetuate these biases when drawing analogies. Overcoming these biases requires not only refining algorithms but also addressing the biases in the training data itself. Ethical considerations are vital in ensuring that analogical reasoning in AI does not reinforce harmful stereotypes or prejudices.

For AI systems to be trusted, they must provide explanations for their conclusions, especially in critical applications like healthcare or law. Developing analogical reasoning methods that generate explanations for the drawn analogies is a significant challenge. Explainable AI is a burgeoning field, striving to make complex AI reasoning processes, including analogical reasoning, transparent and interpretable to humans.

AR is often most effective when combined with other AI techniques like deep learning or reinforcement learning. Integrating these methods seamlessly to enhance analogical reasoning without introducing conflicts or redundancies is a research challenge.

Harmonizing these diverse techniques in a way that augments analogical reasoning capabilities is essential for the development of advanced AI systems.

Ongoing Research Efforts:

Addressing these challenges requires interdisciplinary efforts spanning cognitive psychology, linguistics, computer science, and ethics. Ongoing research focuses on developing AI algorithms that emulate human-like analogical reasoning.

Researchers are exploring advanced machine learning models, including neural networks, to enhance the pattern recognition abilities of AI systems, enabling them to identify subtle similarities and draw accurate analogies.

Enhancements in knowledge representation techniques, such as knowledge graphs and ontologies, are ongoing. These representations aim to capture intricate relationships between entities, facilitating more nuanced analogical reasoning.

Ethical considerations are at the forefront of AI research. Efforts are directed toward mitigating biases in training data and ensuring fairness and transparency in analogical reasoning processes. Integrating explainability into analogical reasoning models is an active area of research.

Developing methods to provide understandable explanations for the drawn analogies enhances the trustworthiness of AI systems. Leveraging human intuition and creativity in conjunction with AI systems is a promising avenue. Human-AI collaboration approaches, where humans and AI jointly solve problems, are being explored to enhance the analogical reasoning capabilities of AI.

• • • •

Analogy-Based Learning.

• • • •

AI systems can not only transfer knowledge effectively but also generate innovative solutions, making them valuable tools in diverse applications. Through analogy-based learning individuals recognize similarities between known concepts and apply them to comprehend new, unfamiliar information.

In artificial intelligence, this process is emulated through specific algorithms and models designed to recognize and utilize analogies effectively. AI systems employing analogy-based learning first need to recognize analogous relationships within the data. This recognition involves identifying shared patterns, structures, or semantic similarities between different sets of information.

For instance, in a linguistic context, recognizing that the relationship between "man" and "woman" is analogous to "king" and "queen" requires understanding the shared gender relationships. Analogical reasoning in AI often involves mapping the knowledge structures of known and unknown concepts.

By aligning these structures based on recognized analogies, AI systems transfer knowledge from familiar concepts to unfamiliar ones. This mapping enables the system to infer new information or make predictions about the unknown based on the known.

Once analogies are recognized and knowledge structures are mapped, analogy-based learning enables AI systems to perform analogical inference. This inference involves applying the relationships and patterns identified in analogous situations to draw conclusions or generate new hypotheses. In cases where certain facts are known, analogical inference can help deduce related facts about unknown situations.

Various AI algorithms are designed to facilitate analogy-based learning. These algorithms often employ techniques from pattern recognition, machine learning, and semantic analysis.

For example, in textual data, word embeddings and vector space models enable the identification of semantic relationships and analogies. Algorithms like k-nearest neighbors (KNN) will be adapted to find similar instances based on recognized analogies.

It assigns a label to a new sample based on the labels of its k closest samples in the training set, does not build a model from the training data, and all of its computation is deferred until the prediction time. The idea behind the KNN classification algorithm is very simple, given a new sample, assign it to the class that is most common among its k nearest neighbors.

KNN is also a very flexible model, it can find decision boundaries of any shape between the classes, and can be used for both classification and regression problems. The idea behind the KNN classification algorithm is very simple: given a new sample, assign it to the class that is most common among its k nearest neighbors.

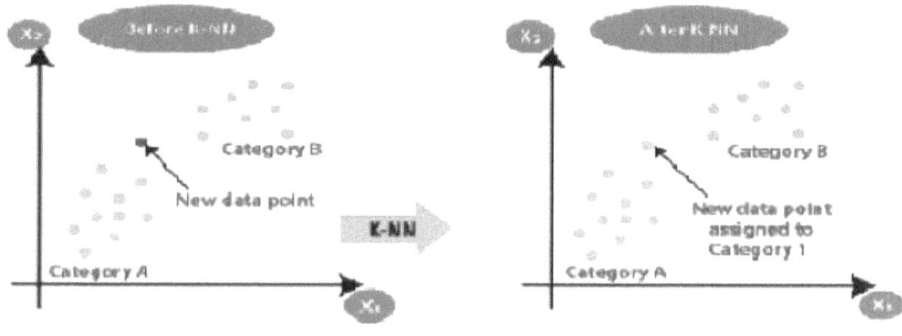

Source: towardsdatascience.com

Researchers in the field of artificial intelligence and cognitive science develop computational models inspired by people cognition. These models, often referred to as cognitive architectures, aim to replicate human-like analogy-based learning processes. By studying people cognition and implementing analogous mechanisms in AI systems, researchers gain insights into how people learn and reason by analogy.

Analogical reasoning is particularly valuable in domain adaptation tasks. In situations where an AI system is trained in one domain but needs to perform in a related, but distinct, domain, recognizing analogies between the two domains aids in transferring knowledge.

Analogical reasoning allows the system to adapt its understanding and predictions from the source to the target domain.

Analogies are at the heart of creative problem-solving. AI systems utilizing analogy-based learning generate creative solutions to problems by drawing analogies from diverse domains. This ability is especially valuable in innovative tasks, such as generating novel designs, composing music, or devising unique strategies in games.

Analogy-based learning finds applications in various fields, including natural language processing, recommendation systems, biomedical research, and robotics. For instance, in recommendation systems, recognizing analogies in user preferences enables the system to suggest items based on similar users' choices, enhancing the personalization of recommendations.

1.3. What can AI bet on in the Context of Cross-cultural Relations?

Could artificial intelligence be the catalyst for positive change in marginalized neighborhoods in Marseille, France, plagued by ongoing threats and riots?. Similarly, could it address the overcrowded conditions in certain areas of New Delhi?.

Can the IA, with its instruments, really help to eradicate these critical situations, both in terms of population and mass displacement, which ultimately lead to problems of coexistence and the maintenance of order within international communities, whether on one continent or another?.

The proliferation of popular mobility tools and apps, alongside an unpredictable digital landscape, often sparks optimism about forthcoming positive developments and desired changes. However, these feelings often amount to little more than hopeful wishes, lacking tangible and substantial transformations in reality. That is where the challenge lies.

In this dynamic, AI acquires value, once it weighs up an environment of interaction and extensive contact, evaluating the various options and, overseeing a reality where ingenuity and minimalism seek their own specific outcomes. Let us skip this extensive contact, highlighting external and internal connections, clarifying as far as possible the different contributions linked to fields of manifest collective interest.

AI-powered language translation tools break down language barriers, facilitating communication and understanding between individuals and groups from different cultures. These tools help people engage in cross-cultural conversations and collaborations more easily.

AI will be used to customize user experiences based on cultural preferences and sensitivities. For example, AI algorithms adjust content recommendations, advertising, and user interfaces to align with the cultural norms and values of specific user groups.

AI-driven educational platforms provide insights into different cultures, helping people learn about and appreciate cultural diversity. These platforms offer language courses, cultural history lessons, and etiquette guides to enhance cross-cultural competence.

AI assist organizations in promoting diversity and inclusion by helping to identify and rectify biases in hiring, promotion, and decision-making processes. AI tools analyze data to ensure that opportunities are equitable across different cultural backgrounds.

AI-driven chatbots and virtual assistants provide real-time cross-cultural communication guidance. These tools offer makes explicit suggestions on appropriate language, gestures, and etiquette when interacting with individuals from different cultures.

AI algorithms analyze user preferences and recommend cultural content such as books, movies, music, and news articles from different parts of the world. This help people broaden their cultural horizons.

AI-powered mediation and conflict resolution tools facilitate peaceful dialogue between parties with cultural differences. These tools provide neutral and culturally sensitive guidance to resolve disputes.

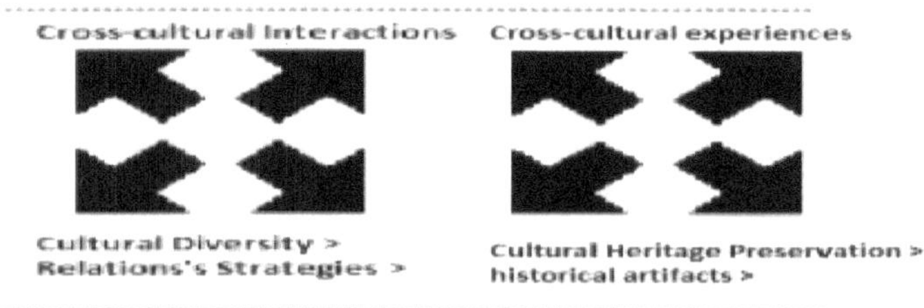

AI aid in the preservation and digitization of cultural heritage, including historical artifacts, texts, and oral traditions. This ensures that cultural knowledge is accessible to future generations. AI-driven travel apps and services provide cultural insights and recommendations to travelers, by supporting them in navigating unfamiliar cultures and make the most of their cross-cultural experiences.

AI build online communities where individuals from diverse backgrounds connect, share experiences, and learn from one another. AI assist in developing and delivering cultural sensitivity training programs for individuals and organizations. These programs raise awareness and reduce misunderstandings in cross-cultural interactions.

AI analyze vast amounts of data related to cross-cultural interactions, identifying trends and areas where cultural misunderstandings or conflicts may arise. This information inform strategies for improved cross-cultural relations.

Nor can we neglect the efforts and activities aimed at safeguarding and maintaining elements of a culture's heritage and identity for future generations, or in other words: 'Cultural heritage preservation'. This heritage includes tangible and intangible aspects of a culture, such as historical artifacts, traditions, rituals, languages, art, literature, music, and more.

AI technologies, such as image recognition and 3D scanning, are utilised to digitize and archive physical artifacts, such as ancient manuscripts, artwork, sculptures, and historical documents. This digitization process creates high-quality digital replicas that will be preserved indefinitely and made accessible to a global audience.

AI-driven speech recognition and transcription tools assist in documenting and preserving endangered languages. Linguists and cultural experts will use these tools to transcribe and archive oral traditions, stories, and songs, helping to ensure the survival of linguistic diversity.

AI collaborates in the organization and management of vast cultural heritage archives. Automated tagging and metadata generation makes it easier to search and retrieve relevant cultural resources within digital archives.

AI-powered image analysis and restoration techniques aid in the restoration and conservation of deteriorating artworks and historical sites. These technologies help restore cultural artifacts to their original condition, preserving their historical and artistic value.

AI facilitates broader access to cultural heritage resources through virtual tours, interactive exhibits, and educational platforms. Virtual reality (VR) and augmented reality (AR) applications make it possible to explore cultural sites and artifacts remotely, fostering greater understanding and appreciation of diverse cultures.

AI-powered translation tools assist in translating ancient texts, inscriptions, and manuscripts into modern languages, making them more accessible to researchers and the public. This aids in the understanding of historical and cultural contexts.

AI examines data related to the preservation needs of cultural heritage sites and artifacts. It identify environmental threats, recommend preservation techniques, and predict potential risks to cultural assets. AI expresses a co-operation in favor of engage local communities and cultural experts in the preservation process. It facilitate collaborative efforts to document and protect cultural traditions and knowledge.

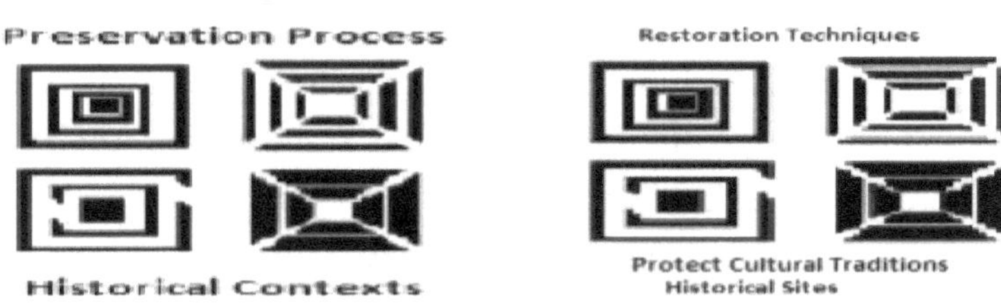

And what about Cultural Sensitivity Training?. We face educational programs and initiatives designed to increase awareness and understanding of cultural differences, foster respect for diversity, and promote effective and respectful cross-cultural interactions.

These training programs aim to equip individuals, organizations, and communities with the knowledge, skills, and attitudes needed to navigate culturally diverse environments and engage with people from different cultural backgrounds.

Cultural sensitivity training begins by clarifying participants become aware of their own cultural biases and assumptions. It encourages individuals to reflect on their own cultural background and how it may influence their perceptions and interactions with others.

The training goes beyond awareness and aims to develop cultural competence, which includes the ability to effectively communicate, collaborate, and relate to individuals from diverse cultural backgrounds. This rationalizes a learning process about different cultural norms, values, customs, and communication styles.

Cultural sensitivity addresses stereotypes and prejudices that lead to misunderstandings and biases. It promotes empathy and challenges stereotypes by providing accurate information about different cultures.

These programs often focus on improving cross-cultural communication skills. This includes learning how to listen actively, ask culturally sensitive questions, and adapt communication styles to the preferences of individuals from different cultures.

Participants in cultural sensitivity training are encouraged to develop cultural intelligence (CQ), which addresses the ability to adapt and work effectively in culturally diverse settings. CQ includes cognitive, motivational, and behavioral aspects. CQ specifically orders the variables of an interface in which the individual is operating in cross-cultural social contexts or in contexts where there are people from diverse cultural backgrounds.

As intercultural competence, CQ has been conceptualised and measured using four factors: motivational, cognitive, metacognitive and behavioural. Motivational CQ focuses on an individual's drive to engage in intercultural interactions despite the challenges posed by cultural differences.

Cognitive CQ focuses on acquiring knowledge about different cultures, including knowledge of cultural values, norms, conventions and practices. Metacognitive CQ focuses on higher-order thinking skills, primarily the ability to adopt a perspective and develop mental schemas that can guide intercultural interactions.

Specifically, it re-emphasizse the point that if there is awareness of cultural differences and individuals show interest and direct their efforts to understanding these differences, them they will adopt the appropiate behavior when interacting with others from different cultural. Thus as businesses continue to operate in the global envirenment, cultural intellligence will play an integral role in their success.

Success will however be dependent on managers' ability to interact with people from different cultures and also their ability to function effectively in cultural diverse situations. A change in managers' perspective on managing in a culturally diverse setting will therefore, be necessary.

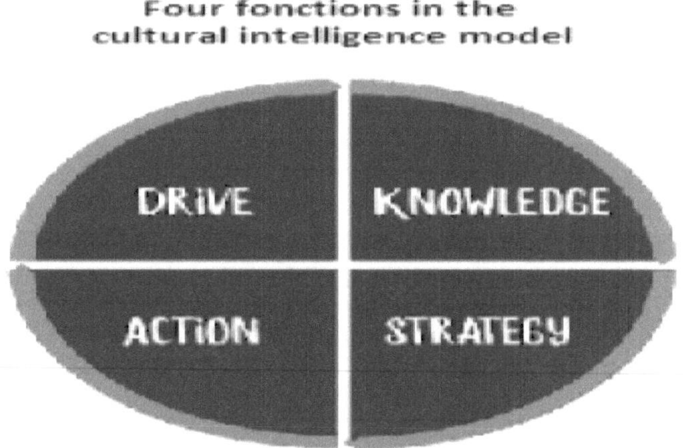

Training often includes real-life case studies and scenarios that illustrate cross-cultural challenges and solutions. Participants analyze these cases and practice applying their cultural sensitivity skills.

Cultural sensitivity training is closely related to broader diversity and inclusion initiatives.

Cultural sensitivity is an ongoing process, and training programs emphasize the importance of continuous learning and self-improvement in this area. Participants are encouraged to stay informed about global cultural developments and trends.

By promoting cultural sensitivity and competence, these training programs aim to reduce cultural misunderstandings, improve cross-cultural collaboration, and create more inclusive and harmonious relationships among individuals and communities with diverse cultural backgrounds.

On the other hand, it is worthwhile in this context to adapt the use of AI algorithms and recommendation systems to suggest cultural content, such as books, movies, music, articles, and other forms of media, to individuals based on their interests and preferences related to different cultures.

This concept is similar to how platforms like Netflix recommend movies or Amazon suggests products, but it focuses specifically on content that engages individuals to explore with various cultural aspects. We are dealing with cultural content recommendations.

AI-driven recommendation systems analyze user data, including past content consumption, ratings, and interactions, to understand an individual's cultural interests and preferences. It then suggests cultural content that aligns with those preferences.

The recommended cultural content span various categories. Suggesting books, novels, poetry, and literature from different cultures and authors. Recommending films and documentaries that explore cultural themes, histories, and traditions. Suggesting music genres, artists, and tracks from around the world, exposing users to different musical traditions.

Recommending art collections, exhibitions, virtual tours of museums, and visual content that showcases diverse artistic traditions.

Providing recipes, cooking tutorials, and content related to international cuisines and culinary traditions. Recommending articles, news stories, and blogs that cover global cultural events, festivals, and developments.

Cultural content recommendations aim to promote cultural learning and enrichment. Users gain insights into the customs, history, languages, and lifestyles of various cultures through the content they consume.

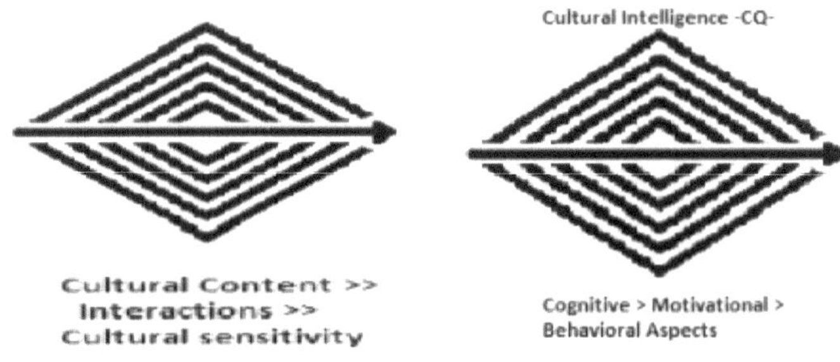

Exposure to diverse cultural content lead to increased cross-cultural understanding and appreciation. It helps individuals develop a broader perspective and empathy for, discussing, and sharing their discoveries with others, fostering meaningful cross-cultural people from different cultural backgrounds.

Cultural content recommendations encourage users to engage in cultural exchange by exploringl interactions. AI algorithms curate cultural content from a vast pool of available resources, making it easier for users to discover content they may not have encountered otherwise.

Recommendation systems often incorporate user feedback and ratings to refine their recommendations, ensuring that the suggested cultural content aligns more closely with the individual's evolving interests.

An algorithm commonly used for content recommendations, including cultural content, is the Collaborative Filtering algorithm.

Collaborative Filtering is a technique that makes automatic predictions about the preferences of a user by collecting preferences from many users (collaborating).

1. User-Item Matrix:

The algorithm begins by creating a matrix that represents the preferences of users for different cultural items (movies, music, books, etc.). Each row corresponds to a user, and each column corresponds to an item. The matrix is filled with ratings or preferences given by users to the items.

```
|| Movie A | Movie B | Movie C | Movie D |
|————-|————-|————-|————-|————-|
| User 1 | 5 | 4 || 3 |
| User 2 || 5 | 4 ||
| User 3 | 4 ||| 5 |
| User 4 ||| 3 ||
```

. . . .

2. User Similarity:

The algorithm calculates the similarity between users based on their preferences. Common metrics for similarity include cosine similarity or Pearson correlation. Users who have similar preferences will have a higher similarity score.

3. Neighborhood Selection:

For a given user, the algorithm selects a neighborhood of similar users based on their calculated similarity scores. This neighborhood represents users whose preferences align closely with the target user.

4. Item Recommendation:

The algorithm identifies items that the users in the neighborhood have liked but the target user has not yet interacted with. These unexplored items are then recommended to the target user.

. . . .

	Movie A	Movie B	Movie C	Movie D
—	—	—	—	—
User 1	5	4	2	3
User 2	3	5	4	1
User 3	4	2	1	5
User 4	2	1	3	4

· · · ·

5. Rating Prediction:

The algorithm predicts the rating that the target user might give to the recommended items based on the ratings given by similar users. The predicted ratings are used to rank the recommended items.

Nor do we ignore the concept of conflict resolution and mediation, through which artificial intelligence technologies and techniques assist in managing and resolving conflicts between individuals, groups, or entities from different cultural backgrounds or in cross-cultural settings. Conflict resolution and mediation are critical aspects of cross-cultural relations, as cultural differences often lead to misunderstandings or disputes.

AI provide support to people mediators by offering tools and resources to facilitate mediation processes. These tools include chatbots or virtual assistants designed to help parties communicate effectively and follow established mediation protocols.

AI-powered language translation and interpretation tools bridge language gaps between parties involved in a conflict. This ensures that everyone express themselves and understand one another, even when they speak different languages.

AI systems are inherently neutral and impartial, which are advantageous in mediating conflicts. They do not have personal biases or emotions that might affect their judgment, they are able to facilitate discussions objectively.

AI examines large sets of data related to the conflict, identifying patterns, underlying causes, and potential solutions. This data-driven approach help mediators make informed decisions during the mediation process. AI algorithms predict the likely outcomes of different conflict resolution strategies based on historical data and the specifics of the current conflict.

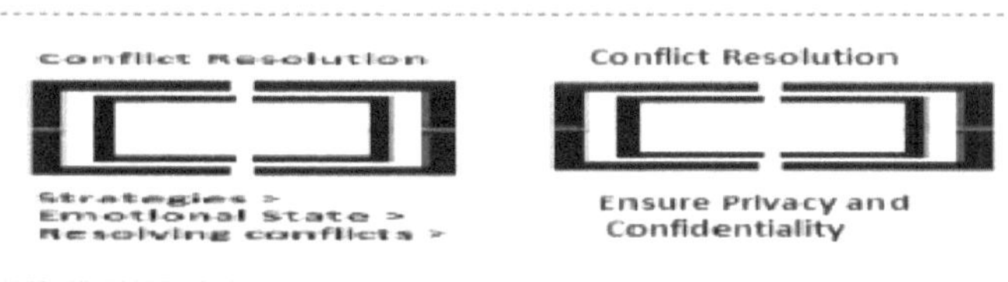

AI assess the nature and severity of a conflict by analyzing text-based or verbal communications between the parties. It identify emotional cues and expressions that might help mediators understand the parties' perspectives better. AI systems are designed to ensure privacy and confidentiality during mediation.

AI power online mediation platforms that provide a secure and accessible environment for parties to engage in conflict resolution discussions. These platforms offer features like secure video conferencing, document sharing, and dispute tracking.

AI has been trained to recognize emotions in spoken or written communication, assisting mediators in calibrating the emotional state of the parties involved and adapting their approach accordingly.

AI systems learn from previous mediation experiences, adapting and improving their mediation techniques over time. This iterative learning process enhance their effectiveness in resolving conflicts. AI also is used proactively to identify potential sources of conflict in cross-cultural interactions and suggest strategies to prevent conflicts from escalating.

In the realm of AI and cross-cultural relations, 'Data Analysis and Insights' involves employing artificial intelligence and data analytics methods to gather, handle, and scrutinize data concerning the interactions among individuals, groups, or entities hailing from diverse cultural backgrounds.

The objective is to derive meaningful insights and patterns from this data to enhance cross-cultural understanding, improve communication, and identify areas for potential conflict resolution.

Data would be collected from various sources, such as communication logs, social media interactions, surveys, and feedback forms. These sources may contain textual data, audio recordings, or even video content that captures cross-cultural interactions.

AI analyze textual data, such as emails, chat logs, or social media posts, to identify sentiment, emotional tone, and key themes related to cross-cultural interactions. This analysis can reveal patterns of misunderstanding, frustration, or positive engagement.

Natural language processing (NLP) techniques are applied to understand and process text in different languages, enabling analysis of interactions between individuals who speak different languages.of cross-cultural interactions. For example, it analyze the spoken words, facial expressions, and tone of voice during video conferences.

AI combine and analyze data from multiple modalities, including text, audio, and video, to gain a more comprehensive understanding. AI algorithms identify recurring patterns and behaviors in cross-cultural interactions. For instance, they detect common challenges in communication, areas of cultural sensitivity, or topics that frequently lead to misunderstandings.

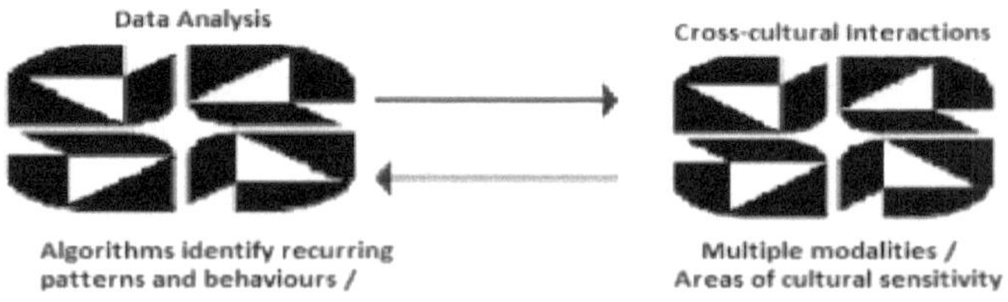

Over time, AI track changes in sentiment and communication dynamics within cross-cultural relationships. This tracking help identify shifts in attitudes and potential sources of tension or improvement. AI analyze communication styles, such as directness, formality, or use of honorifics, in cross-cultural interactions.

AI identify potential conflicts or disputes based on language patterns, emotional cues, or changes in communication dynamics. Early detection enable timely intervention or mediation. Based on data analysis, AI provide recommendations for improving cross-cultural interactions. These recommendations may include language adjustments, cultural sensitivity training, or suggested conflict resolution strategies.

AI create visual representations and dashboards that present data insights in a user-friendly format. These visualizations are designed to make it easy for individuals and organizations easily understand and act upon the data. Advanced AI models use historical data to make predictions about future cross-cultural interactions. For example, they predict potential conflict hotspots or areas where cultural adaptation may be necessary.

If we discuss artificial intelligence and digital platforms, to create and foster online communities where individuals from diverse cultural backgrounds connect, collaborate, share experiences, and build meaningful relationships, we are focusing on the concept of Community Building, in the context of AI and cross-cultural relations. These communities are designed to facilitate cross-cultural interactions, enhance understanding, and promote unity among members.

AI-powered platforms, websites, or social networks are created to serve as virtual spaces for cross-cultural community building. These platforms are designed to be inclusive and user-friendly, encouraging participation from individuals of various cultural backgrounds. AI algorithms match individuals with common interests, goals, or hobbies, regardless of their cultural background.

Community-building platforms often include discussion forums, interest-based groups, and topic-specific communities. These spaces are a place for members to engage in conversations, ask questions, and share insights on various subjects.

Community building aims to promote cultural exchange by encouraging members to share their cultural traditions, stories, festivals, and experiences with others. This exchange fosters cross-cultural understanding and appreciation. The community-building platforms provide guidelines and resources for maintaining cultural sensitivity in interactions

.

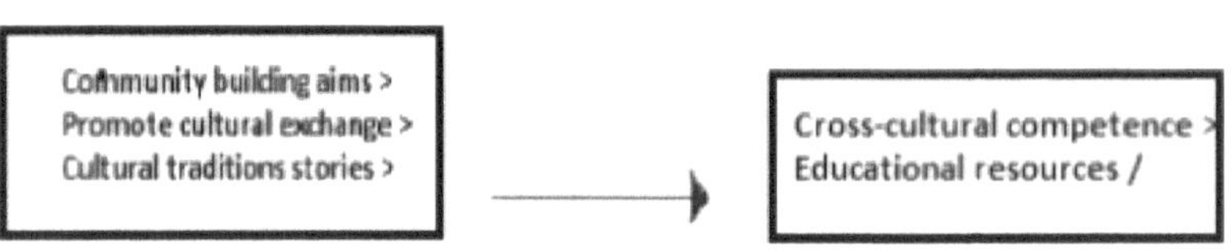

AI assist in organizing virtual events, webinars, workshops, and cultural exchange activities within the community. These events create opportunities for members to learn about and engage with different cultures. AI tools assist in content moderation to ensure a safe and respectful environment for all members. They identify and address inappropriate or offensive content and provide conflict resolution support.

Community-building platforms offer educational resources related to cross-cultural communication, cultural diversity, and global perspectives. These resources help members develop cross-cultural competence. AI collect feedback from community members to continuously improve the platform and its features.

Some community-building initiatives focus on facilitating cross-cultural collaborations, such as joint projects, research endeavors, or social initiatives, where members from different cultures work together for a common goal. Community building emphasizes the celebration of diversity as a strength.

Let us now look at some basic aspects of 'Travel and Tourism Assistance' and what is involved in the use of artificial intelligence technologies to enhance the travel and tourism experience for individuals exploring different cultures and destinations. AI provide a range of services and support to travelers, helping them navigate, and make the most of their cross-cultural travel experiences.

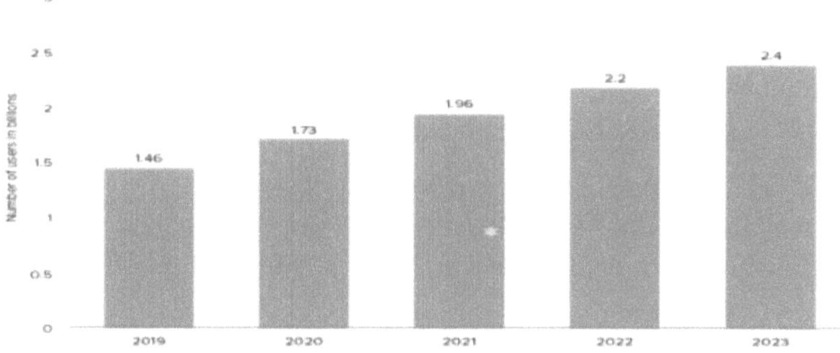

Here are the three main types AR implementations of Travel Applications:

* Location-based AR, also known as geolocation AR, leverages GPS data to overlay virtual content on the user's real-world surroundings. Travel apps equipped with location-based AR identify a user's location and provide relevant information about nearby landmarks, attractions, restaurants, as well as points of interest.

Imagine strolling through a charming city, and as we point your smartphone towards historical monuments, the app instantly displays historical facts, architectural details, as well as user reviews—all in real-time. Thus, this type of AR enhances travelers' understanding of their surroundings and adds an extra layer of excitement to their journey.

* Marker-based AR involves using predefined visual markers, such as QR codes or image recognition, to trigger the display of augmented content. In travel apps, these markers can be strategically placed at specific locations or landmarks.

When users scan these markers with their devices, the app recognizes them and overlays relevant virtual information. For example, a museum could have markers next to each exhibit, and visitors scan them to unlock interactive displays, historical videos, or 3D models related to the artifacts.

Marker-based AR adds a sense of interactivity and engagement, consequently, enabling travelers to unlock hidden experiences with a simple scan.

* SLAM AR (Simultaneous Localization and Mapping) is the most advanced and immersive type of AR, combining real-time location tracking with environmental mapping. Consequently, this technology allows users to explore AR experiences without the need for markers or pre-existing data.

Instead, the app dynamically builds a map of the environment while simultaneously tracking the user's movements within it. For travel apps, this means users can interact with virtual elements in any space they choose to explore, from hotel rooms and city streets to natural landscapes.

Examples of AR Apps in Travel and Tourism are Google Arts & Culture, Wander, HoloLens Tour Guide, AirPano and Augmented Reality City.

To develop augmented reality (AR) apps for travel and tourism, you will need a suitable technology stack that enables the creation of interactive as well as immersive experiences. A list of essential components for building AR apps in this domain:

- Choose an AR development platform that provides tools and libraries to create AR experiences. Some popular choices WILL include, ARKit (for iOS); Apple's

- Integrate location-based services to enhance the travel and tourism experience. This can be done using APIs like, Google Maps API; Mapbox SDK.

- Implement geolocation to determine the user's current location and provide relevant AR content based on their surroundings.

-To recognize real-world objects or images, we'll need computer vision libraries like, OpenCV, TensorFlow Lite.

- Set up a server to handle user data, preferences, and interactions. Common technologies for backend development include, Node.js; Django; Ruby on Rails

- Choose a database to store user-related information and app data. Options include, MySQL; PostgreSQL or MongoDB.

AI-powered travel platforms and apps help travelers plan their trips to culturally diverse destinations. These platforms suggest itineraries, recommend cultural attractions, and provide information on visa requirements, local customs, and cultural events. AI-based translation tools and mobile apps can assist travelers in communicating with local residents in different languages.

AI provides travelers with information on cultural nuances, etiquette, and traditions of the destinations they plan to visit. This information facilitates travelers show respect for local customs and engage more meaningfully with the local culture.

AI-driven navigation and mapping services provide real-time guidance to travelers, helping them explore cities, historical sites, and cultural landmarks with ease. These tools also recommend public transportation options and routes.

AI apps recommend local restaurants, provide information on cuisine types, and even offer menu translations. Travelers explore and savor the diverse culinary offerings of their destination culture. AI provide real-time safety information, including updates on political situations, weather conditions, and health advisories. This ensures that travelers make informed decisions about their safety and well-being.

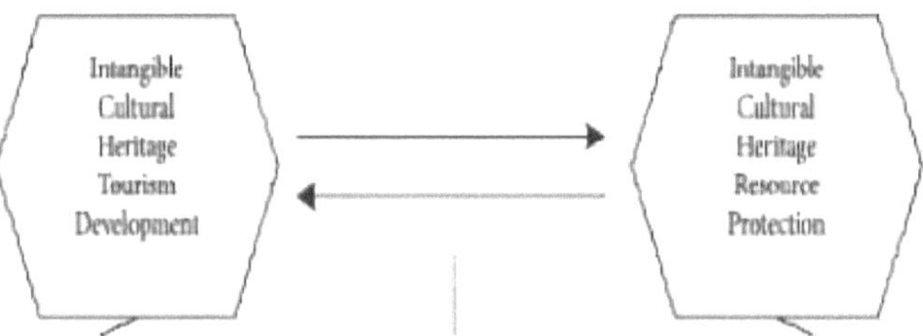

AI algorithms analyze travellers' preferences and past behavior to offer personalized recommendations for cultural experiences, activities, and attractions based on their interests. AI-powered virtual guides and tour apps provide travelers with narrated tours of cultural sites, historical landmarks, museums, and more, offering cultural context and historical background.

AI assist travelers in cross-cultural interactions by offering language translation and cultural etiquette tips. This is particularly positive when engaging with local residents, artisans, or tour guides. Then, enhance accessibility for travelers with disabilities by providing information on accessible accommodations, transportation, and cultural sites.

The use of artificial intelligence technologies will also be associated with improve and facilitate communication between individuals or groups from different cultural backgrounds. The goal is to enhance understanding, minimize misunderstandings, and foster more effective and respectful interactions in cross-cultural settings.

Overall, cross-cultural communication enhancement through AI aims to bridge linguistic and cultural gaps, promote effective communication, and encourage respectful interactions among individuals or groups from diverse cultural backgrounds.

AI-driven language translation tools automatically translate spoken or written communication between languages, making it easier for individuals who speak different languages to communicate. These tools handle real-time translation in conversations or translate written documents.

AI provide cultural context to aid in communication. For example, it offer insights into cultural norms, taboos, and etiquette, helping individuals understand the cultural implications of their words and actions.

AI offer suggestions for culturally sensitive language and behaviors. It provide real-time feedback to users, suggesting alternative phrases or communication styles that are more respectful in a given cultural context. AI-based language learning tools help individuals improve their pronunciation and reduce language barriers. These tools provide personalized feedback on accent and articulation.

However, a literal translation of this expression into another language may not effectively convey the intended message. Similarly, it may result in translations that are considered technically accurate but do not effectively convey the intended meaning.

Therefore, in order to achieve an accurate translation of the aforementioned expression, it is imperative that the translation tool has a comprehensive understanding of the contextual and cultural implications associated with the expression.

Consequently, this study aims to highlight and explore how these AI-based translation tools can be creatively used to properly facilitate cross-cultural communication.

The process of translation always involves both linguistic and cultural elements, as these two aspects are inherently intertwined and cannot be separated. The cultural embedding of language is a phenomenon whereby language serves as a means of expressing and shaping cultural reality.

The interpretation of linguistic elements depends on the specific culture in which they are used and cannot be fully understood in isolation from this context. It is imperative for translators to carefully consider the differences in practices and levels of standardisation between the source and target cultures when transferring a written work from one cultural context to another.

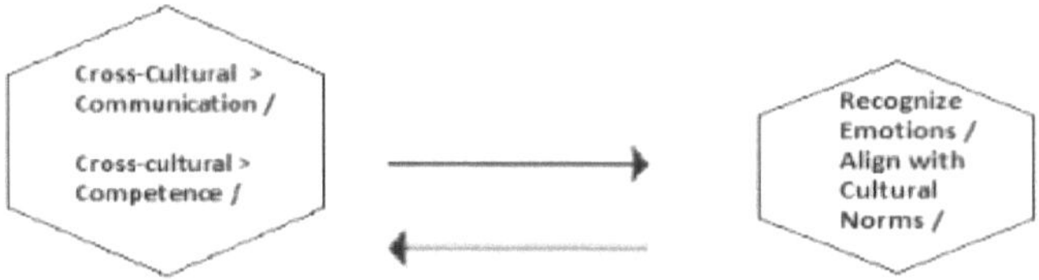

Despite the overwhelming body of research on the use of AI-based translation technology to address cross-cultural communication, there are still a number of issues and concerns that need to be addressed.

There are several critical concerns regarding AI translations, such as the perspectives of language experts and professional translators on the issue of accuracy and excellence of translations, the likely loss of subtlety and cultural context during the translation process, the potential influence on translators and the translation field, and the ethical and societal consequences of relying on AI for cross-cultural communication.

The lack of shared cultural characteristics poses a significant challenge to intercultural communication, making translation an insurmountable task. When discussing the translation of two languages with equivalent meanings, "it is necessary for translators to effectively convey the same referential, pragmatic and interrelated meanings".

In essence, the act of translation requires the translator to take into account the specific circumstances and cultural milieu of both the source and target cultures in order to produce a translation that is comprehensible on multiple levels.

AI versatilizes communication styles and preferences of individuals from different cultures and pushing users adapt their communication style to better align with those preferences. For example, it suggest more direct or indirect communication approaches based on cultural norms. AI identify grammatical errors, vocabulary misuse, and pronunciation mistakes, by offering users the option to communicate more effectively and professionally in a foreign language.

AI-powered platforms enable multilingual communication in various settings, such as business meetings, conferences, or social interactions. These platforms facilitate real-time language translation for participants. AI-driven e-learning modules and courses provide individuals with cultural awareness and sensitivity training, in order to enhance cross-cultural competence.

AI provide users with feedback and assessments on their cross-cultural communication skills. It track progress and suggest areas for improvement over time. AI analyze vocal cues and facial expressions to recognize emotions during cross-cultural conversations.

AI inspects the text-based or voice-based communication to identify patterns, common misunderstandings, and areas where cultural adaptation may be necessary. This analysis offer insights for improved communication. AI assist in resolving conflicts that arise due to cultural misunderstandings by providing suggestions for conflict resolution strategies that align with the cultural context.

Different cultures have different communication norms that establish criteria for what is considered acceptable and unacceptable. In some cultural contexts, individuals show respect by avoiding direct eye contact with their interlocutor. In different cultural contexts, avoiding eye contact may indicate a lack of interest. This is because each culture has its own norms and expectations.

'Cultural Sensitivity and Customization' is about to promote cultural awareness and adapt digital experiences, products, and services to align with the cultural norms, values, and preferences of specific user groups. In this context, AI collect user data, including cultural background, language preferences, and geographic location, to create user profiles, for the understanding the cultural context of each user.

AI algorithms tailor content recommendations, user interfaces, and digital experiences to match the cultural preferences of individual users or specific cultural groups. For example, an AI-powered news app prioritize news articles from a user's home country or region.

Each learning environment poses unique challenges and requirements, and a single approach may not be efficiently adapted to all situations. It is therefore important to recognise the relevance of contextual adaptability and the need for flexible and customisable AI technologies to meet different educational needs.

Schools should have the flexibility to customise AI tools based on their specific needs or preferences. This approach empowers more schools and institutions to utilise AI-based solutions more efficiently and effectively (tailor-made AI solutions).

As the modern educational landscape evolves, it is imperative to understand that best practices may vary from one environment to another. This makes it essential to foster a culture of innovation to build contextual adaptations that streamline AI technologies for maximum impact (innovative adaptations).

Socio-economic factors, geographic locations and other contextual variables can impact educational environments significantly. AI-based tools must be customisable to address these unique challenges, while maintaining academic quality and supporting student learning (Adapting to context-specific challenges).

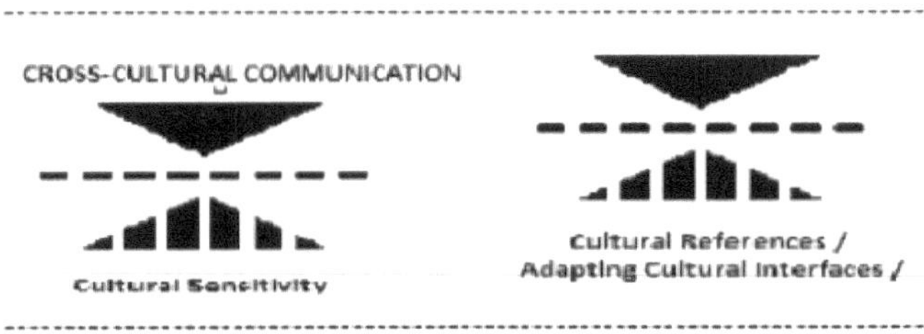

Returning to the initial aspects, AI automatically detect a user's language and location and provide content in the user's preferred language. It also offer localized content, such as news, weather updates, and recommendations that are relevant to the user's geographic location.

Then proposes cultural insights and tips to users when they engage with content or services from a different culture. These insights may include explanations of cultural references, etiquette guidelines, and explanations of symbolism.

AI inform users about important cultural events, holidays, and celebrations relevant to their cultural background or the region they are in. This information enhance cultural understanding and encourage participation. AI recommend products, services, and content that align with the cultural interests and values of users. For instance, it suggest movies, books, or music from a user's culture.

AI systems learn from user feedback and preferences to continually refine their customization. Over time, AI better understand each user's unique cultural sensitivities and adapt accordingly. In educational contexts, AI provide customized cultural sensitivity training modules and resources to individuals or organizations.

AI assist in tailoring marketing campaigns and advertisements to different cultural segments. This ensures that advertising messages are culturally relevant and sensitive. AI ensure that digital platforms and services are accessible and inclusive for users from various cultural backgrounds, including those with disabilities.

Examples: Film and television production companies actively cast actors from various cultural backgrounds and create storylines that authentically represent the diversity of cultures. Advertisers use inclusive imagery that resonates with different cultural groups.

'Cultural Education and Awareness' guides us to the use of artificial intelligence technologies to provide educational resources, insights, and experiences that enhance individuals' understanding of different cultures, traditions, and global diversity. The goal here, is to promote cultural awareness, appreciation, and cross-cultural competence.

AI-powered educational platforms and apps offer courses, lessons, and resources that teach users about various cultures, their histories, languages, traditions, and customs. These platforms can cater to learners of all ages and backgrounds.

AI-driven language learning apps help users acquire proficiency in different languages, enabling them to engage more effectively with people from diverse cultural backgrounds, often incorporating voice recognition and personalised lessons.

AI provide access to digital archives, historical documents, and virtual exhibits that showcase the cultural history and heritage of different societies. Users explore artifacts, artworks, and texts from around the world. AI create interactive simulations and virtual experiences that immerse users in different cultural contexts. For example, virtual reality (VR) or augmented reality (AR) apps transport users to historical periods or cultural events.

The main difference between AR and VR is that the former adds virtual elements to the real world, while the latter creates an entirely new virtual world that users can immerse themselves in and explore. In other words, virtual reality creates a fully immersive and artificial experience, while augmented reality adds digital information to the existing physical experience.

Advantages of Augmented Reality: Improves user experience, allows users to interact with virtual objects in a real environment, improving the user experience. Increases efficiency, as it help to increase efficiency in a wide variety of sectors such as industry, medicine, construction, tourism, education, advertising, marketing, entertainment, retail, etc., by providing real-time information.

It reduces costs in the production of products and services by letting users see what they will look like and work before they are mass-produced. Facilitates learning and makes it more interactive and engaging by offering users interact with virtual objects in a real environment.

It creates new business opportunities. Augmented reality will be an effective marketing tool, companies will create interactive and engaging advertising campaigns. It also facilitates the visualisation of products and services, which can, among other benefits, increase a company's sales.

Disadvantages of Augmented Reality: It requires specific hardware. To experience augmented reality, we will need a compatible device, such as a smartphone or tablet, which may limit its use, although it is true that it is more accessible than other technologies as it can be consumed simply with a mobile phone, without the need for other specific devices.

It may cause dizziness or nausea in some people, especially if used for long periods of time. The accuracy of the overlay of virtual elements may be limited depending on the capabilities of the device used.

Creating high quality augmented reality experiences can be expensive, which may limit their use for smaller companies. For example, at Onirix this is one of the barriers we overcome with our no-code / low-code platform, as anyone can create a professional augmented reality experience without the need for technical knowledge or high investment.

Augmented Reality (AR) uses a mix of advanced technologies. Computer vision algorithms analyse and understand real-world visual input, while tracking systems identify the location and orientation of the device. Virtual material is superimposed on the user's vision through display technologies such as head-mounted displays or smartphones.

Sensors capture the real-world environment and provide depth information, motion detection and position tracking. High-performance graphics processing units (GPUs) create realistic 3D visuals, while software development kits (SDKs) provide tools for developing AR applications.

These technologies work together to seamlessly combine digital information with the real world, enhancing the user's perception and engagement with their environment.

Example: Snapchat launched so-called augmented reality filters, which enables users to add virtual features to their selfies, such as masks, animations and effects. According to Creative Marketing LTD, Snapchat announced in an investor presentation that more than 250 million (63%) of the platform's daily active users engage with reality augmented features such as filters. These filters have become very popular, inspiring other social networks to implement similar AR features, such as Instagram, Facebook and TikTok.

With Augmented Reality, traders may construct virtual showrooms where customers can explore and visualize products in their own space. For example, the furniture retail company IKEA released 'IKEA Place', which enables customers to see how a particular sofa or table will look in their living room. They virtually place 3D models of furniture in their environment, adjust sizes, colors, and styles providing a more immersive and personalized shopping experience.

AI offer guidance on cultural etiquette, including proper behavior, gestures, and customs when interacting with people from specific cultures. This helps users avoid unintentional cultural misunderstandings. AI platforms provide information about cultural festivals, holidays, and celebrations worldwide. Users learn about the significance of these events and even participate in virtual celebrations.

AI teach users about the geography of different regions, including their physical landscapes, climate, and geographical features. This knowledge provides context for understanding cultural practices and lifestyles. For example, Google Maps is an application that uses 2D data to provide navigational routes to its users, while GPS devices give us detailed geographic information.

AI-driven news aggregators and platforms curate international news, ensuring that users stay informed about global events, cultural developments, and international affairs. In educational and professional contexts, AI raises training programs that teach individuals how to communicate effectively and respectfully in cross-cultural situations.

Language Translation and Understanding.

Machine Translation (MT) is a subfield of computational linguistics that focuses on the automated translation of text or speech from one language to another. The primary goal of machine translation is to simplify and speed up the process of translating content while maintaining a high level of accuracy. MT systems can be classified into three main types: Rule-Based Machine Translation (RBMT), Statistical Machine Translation (SMT), and Neural Machine Translation (NMT).

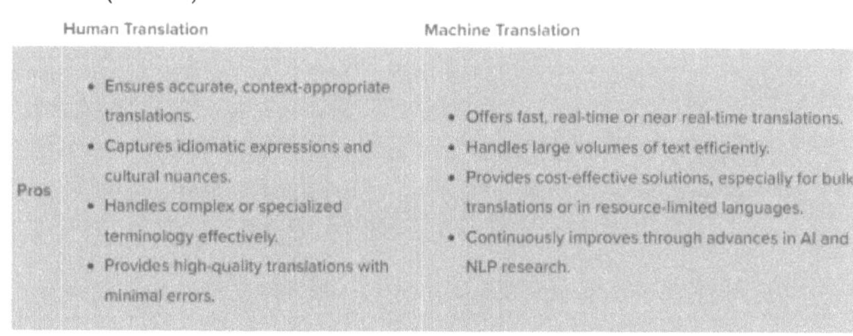

Machine Translation Approaches: Direct Translation, Transfer-Based Translation and Interlingua-Based Translation.

The Direct Translation approach works by translating the source language directly into the target language, without any intermediate representation. This method often operates at the word or phrase level, using dictionaries and rules to handle lexical, morphological, and syntactic differences between languages. While this approach result in speedy translations, it can also lead to inaccuracies and difficulties in coping with complex language structures.

The Transfer-Based Translation approach involves converting the source language into an intermediate representation that captures its syntactic and semantic structure. This intermediate representation is then used to generate a translation in the target language, subsequently processed through linguistic rules and transformations.

Although typically more computationally expensive than direct translation, transfer-based translation produce higher-quality translations by preserving the structure and meaning of the source text.

The Interlingua-Based Translation approach translates the source language into an abstract, language-independent representation called "interlingua." The target language translation is then generated from the interlingua.

This approach is advantageous for multilingual translation scenarios, as only two translation steps are needed between any pair of languages. However, creating a comprehensive interlingua that can express different language structures accurately is a challenging task.

Cons	<ul><li>Can be more time-consuming, especially for large volumes of text.</li><li>Higher cost compared to machine translation.</li><li>Difficult to scale up to meet increased demand.</li><li>Productivity may depend on individual translator capabilities and expertise.</li></ul>	<ul><li>Prone to errors, including lexical, syntactic, and semantic mistakes.</li><li>May struggle with idioms, cultural nuances, and figurative language.</li><li>Accuracy and fluency can be affected by the quality and volume of training data.</li><li>May not handle complex, domain-specific terminology effectively without fine-tuning.</li></ul>

AI-powered translation tools provide real-time translation of spoken language during conversations, making it possible for individuals who speak different languages to communicate effectively. These tools are often used in settings like international business meetings or travel. AI translate written text, including documents, emails, websites, and chat messages, from one language to another.

AI-driven chatbots and virtual assistants communicate with users in multiple languages. They understand user queries in different languages and respond in the user's preferred language. AI automatically detect the language in which a text or spoken conversation is being conducted.

Advanced AI models recognize cultural nuances and idiomatic expressions in languages, ensuring that translations are not only accurate but also culturally appropriate. AI-powered language learning apps and platforms pushes the individuals acquire proficiency in different languages.

AI transcribe spoken language into text and provide subtitles or captions in different languages for audio and video content. This makes multimedia content more accessible to a global audience. Content creators use AI to generate content in multiple languages, reaching a broader audience and facilitating cross-cultural communication.

AI-driven customer service chatbots and virtual agents provide support in multiple languages, ensuring that customers from different regions access assistance in their preferred language. AI language models, like GPT-3 understand and generate human-like text in multiple languages.

AI assist in professional translation services by automating parts of the translation process. Translation tools are used by human translators to improve efficiency and accuracy. AI generates more options in the preservation of endangered languages by transcribing and translating oral traditions, stories, and documents into more widely spoken languages, helping to document and archive cultural heritage.

Example: ChatGPT, the AI model play a role in language preservation and will be able to document and translate texts and recordings in endangered languages. Linguists and researchers embrace AI models like ChatGPT to transcribe and translate texts, making it easier to create digital archives of these languages.

It is important to differentiate between Machine Translation (MT) and Computer-Assisted Translation (CAT) as they serve distinct purposes and operate on different principles.

Machine Translation (MT): This refers to the automated process of translating text from one language to another using computer algorithms and linguistic models. MT systems operate independently and produce translations without human intervention.

Computer-Assisted Translation (CAT): These are software tools used to assist people translators in their work, streamlining the translation process and enhancing productivity. CAT tools do not provide fully automated translations but rather support the translator in various ways, such as Translation Memory, terminology management, and proofreading tools.

CAT tools typically result in higher-quality translations as human translators maintain control over the translated content, ensuring proper handling of nuances, idioms, and domain-specific terminology.

Machine translation is generally faster than CAT as it generates translations automatically, often in real-time or near real-time. However, the final quality might require post-editing by a human translator to ensure accuracy and fluency.

MT is generally more cost-effective for bulk translation tasks, whereas CAT tools are considered an investment for professional translators who require specialized features and functions.

Machine translation is suitable for quick translations of general content, while CAT tools are more appropriate for professional translators who work on complex, domain-specific texts. CAT tools examples are Microsoft Translator, SDL Trados, and MemoQ.

On another front, AI-powered language learning apps are created to teach endangered languages. These apps provide interactive lessons, pronunciation guidance, and practice exercises, making it more accessible for people to learn and use these languages.

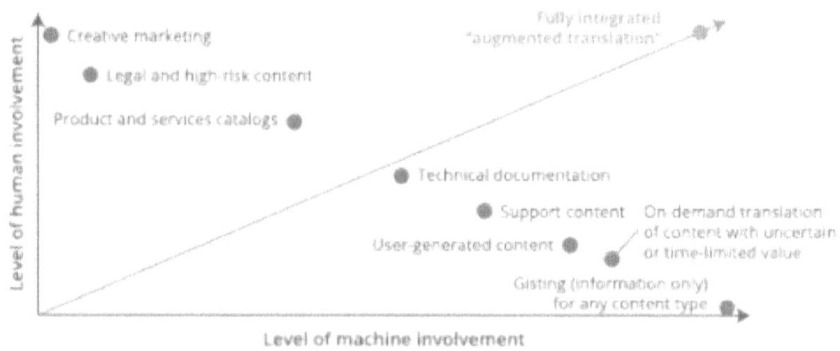

AI is able to automatically generate subtitles and captions in endangered languages for videos and audio recordings. This is very interested in making content more inclusive and accessible to speakers of the endangered language; moreover drive the process to transcribe and analyze oral traditions, such as stories, songs, and folklore, in endangered languages. It will be easier to preserve cultural heritage and pass down traditional knowledge.

AI-based speech recognition systems transcribe spoken words in endangered languages, making it easier to create written records. AI and natural language processing tools assist linguists and researchers in analyzing the grammar, syntax, and vocabulary of endangered languages, aiding in linguistic research and preservation efforts.

SECOND PART

2. Artificial Intelligence in the Financial's Context

Artificial Intelligence (AI) has undeniably ushered in a profound transformation within the financial industry, reshaping its landscape in multifaceted ways. This technological evolution has given rise to diverse perspectives on the role of AI in finance, touching upon not only operational efficiencies and risk management but also redefining customer interactions, market dynamics, and the very nature of financial decision-making. As AI continues to advance, its influence permeates through different layers of the financial sector, prompting reflections on its implications, challenges, and the unprecedented opportunities it brings to the forefront of modern finance.

2.1. Diverse Perspectives on the Role of AI in Finance

Risk Management and Fraud Detection.

• • • •

AI algorithms handle vast amounts of data in real-time, enabling more accurate risk assessments. It enhances fraud detection by identifying unusual patterns or behaviors, contributing to a more secure financial environment. The reliance on AI for risk management raises questions about the potential for algorithmic bias and the need for transparent, ethical AI practices to avoid unintended consequences.

AI algorithms run transaction data in real-time to identify unusual patterns or behaviors that may indicate fraudulent activity. For instance, if a credit card is suddenly used for transactions in multiple countries within a short timeframe, or if there are unusually large transactions that deviate from a customer's typical spending behavior, the system flag these transactions for further investigation.

AI is used in AML efforts to detect patterns associated with money laundering activities. Machine learning models perform vast amounts of transaction data and identify complex, non-obvious relationships between entities. This helps financial institutions comply with Anti-Money Laundering (AML) regulations by automatically flagging suspicious transactions and ensuring timely reporting to regulatory authorities.

Examples: Darktrace, Cylance, Symantec. These platforms use artificial intelligence to dissect patterns of behaviour on the network and detect potential cyber threats, contributing to the security of financial data. Hadoop, Apache Spark, Apache Flink, enable the efficient processing and utilization of large volumes of data, which is critical for risk management and fraud detection. TensorFlow, PyTorch, scikit-learn. Elasticsearch, Kibana, Splunk, would be along the same lines.

The Darktrace case: The detection of insider threats, industrial espionage, IoT compromises, zero-day malware, data loss, supply chain risk, and long-term infrastructure vulnerabilities. The detection of network events using machine learning algorithms. Continual AI-based monitoring of the network and connected devices. Extensive logging details. Scalability, integration, and easy deployment.

• • • •

Algorithmic Trading.

• • • •

AI-driven algorithms execute trades at speeds and frequencies impossible for humans, optimizing trading strategies and enhancing market efficiency. The rapid pace of algorithmic trading contribute to market volatility, and there is a need for regulation to prevent potential systemic risks and ensure fair market practices.

AI algorithms analyze historical trading data to identify patterns and trends. Traders and fund managers use this information to make more informed decisions, manage investment portfolios, and mitigate risks associated with market fluctuations. Machine learning models adapt to changing market conditions and learn from new data, providing valuable insights for trading strategies.

Examples: RapidMiner, IBM SPSS Modeler. These tools empower financial analysts and data scientists to develop predictive models that assist in identifying market trends and making informed decisions.

RapidMiner states the 3 Key Aspects of Creating an Enterprise AI Strategy:

1. The first leg of the stool for any enterprise AI strategy is a leadership team that's deeply committed to leading the initiative. This doesn't mean they've simply signed off on a plan from someone on

their team; they must be personally invested in the cause and willing to dedicate time and effort to drive change across the organization. A comprehensive enterprise AI strategy requires commitment from the top-down.

At RapidMiner, they are fond of saying that data science is a team sport—and every team needs a coach who can make a plan and help each contributor reach their goals. Without a clear play-by-play strategy planned out with know-how from the top, we are going to be stuck in the bush leagues, while your competitors are competing for championships.

Without clear alignment and consistent direction from the entire leadership team, it's just not possible to get everything in place to truly transform an organization with the power of AI and ML.

2. Transforming the way that our company does business with AI and ML is only possible if you give employees the tools and resources that they need to be able to execute on projects in support of our high-level initiative. That means tools that are easy to understand, use, and integrate with the systems that we already have in place—a comprehensive enterprise data science platform.

Hiring a domain expert with strong coding skills is a stretch—hiring a full team of them is a pipe dream. We need tooling that lets people with diverse backgrounds and skills build change cooperatively, playing to their strengths and encouraging collaboration rather than silos.

3. Providing tooling alone isn't enough to succeed, though—we need to change our company culture and evolve the way your employees view their workflows and decision-making. Then, make sure they can productively use the tools that we have implemented.

This involves hands-on tasks and training that let our employees improve their data skills and learn how they can meaningfully contribute to analytics projects. We call this upskilling, and it's an absolutely critical part of any enterprise AI strategy.

Let us return to the previous path. High-frequency trading involves executing a large number of orders at extremely high speeds. AI algorithms, often powered by machine learning, are capable of making split-second decisions and executing trades in microseconds, taking advantage of small price differentials in the market.

AI algorithms play a role in market making, where traders continuously provide buy and sell quotes to create liquidity. These algorithms assess market conditions, bid-ask spreads, and order book dynamics to determine optimal pricing for trades.

Sentiment analysis using natural language processing (NLP) improves the ability to measure market sentiment by analyzing news articles, social media, and other textual data. AI algorithms determine the overall sentiment and adjust trading strategies accordingly, especially in response to news events or public opinion shifts.

AI is integral to assessing and managing risks in algorithmic trading. Machine learning models can predict potential losses, set stop-loss limits, and dynamically adjust position sizes to control risk. This helps algorithmic traders adhere to predefined risk parameters.

AI algorithms are employed for smart order routing, determining the optimal execution venue for trades. They consider factors such as liquidity, transaction costs, and market impact to ensure trades are executed efficiently and at the best available prices.

AI assists in portfolio optimization by dynamically allocating assets based on market conditions and risk-return profiles. Machine learning models analyze correlations between different assets and adjust portfolio weights to maximize returns while minimizing risk.

Algorithmic trading systems with AI capabilities adapt to changing market conditions. Machine learning models continuously learn from new data, allowing algorithms to evolve and adjust strategies in response to evolving market dynamics.

Examples of AI in Algorithmic Trading. Quantitative Hedge Funds:

Renaissance Technologies' Medallion Fund uses sophisticated AI models and quantitative strategies to achieve consistently high returns. The fund employs machine learning techniques to examine vast amounts of financial data and make trading decisions.

Virtu Financial is a prominent high-frequency trading firm that utilizes advanced algorithms, including machine learning models, to execute trades at ultra-fast speeds. These algorithms assess market conditions and execute thousands of trades per second.

Hedge funds and institutional traders use sentiment analysis tools, like those offered by RavenPack, to incorporate news sentiment into their trading algorithms. These tools use NLP to extract sentiment from news articles, social media, and other sources.

AI-Based Robo-Advisors:

Robo-advisors like Wealthfront and Betterment use AI algorithms to automate portfolio management and execute trades on behalf of individual investors. These algorithms consider the investor's risk tolerance, financial goals, and market conditions to optimize portfolio allocations.

AlgoTrader is a platform that utilizes AI for smart order routing. It considers various factors, including liquidity and transaction costs, to determine the optimal execution venue for trades in real-time.

Axioma Risk is a risk management platform that employs AI for assessing portfolio risk. It uses advanced analytics and machine learning to model potential risk scenarios and help asset managers optimize their portfolios in line with risk constraints.

• • • •

Risk measures, application and data integration

RISK MEASURES	MODEL SUPPORT
· Factor sensitivities	· Factor model risk simulations
· Fixed income risk measures	· Market factor risk simulations
· Portfolio aggregation by risk factor	· Linear risk modeling
· Greek sensitivities	· Simulation-based risk modeling of non-linear assets
· Beta	
· Fixed-income valuation measures	· Multiple distribution assumptions available (for example, allowing fat tails to be created)
· Asset aging within scenarios	
· Multi-currency support	· Independent settings for correlation and volatility estimation
· Multi-horizon support	
· Statistical measures	

••••

Customer Service and Personalization.

••••

AI-powered chatbots and virtual assistants provide efficient and personalized customer service, improving user experience and reducing response times. There is a balance to strike between automation and maintaining a people touch in customer interactions. Privacy concerns also arise as AI systems handle sensitive financial information.

AI-powered sentiment analysis will be applied to news articles, social media, and other textual data to gauge market sentiment. By understanding the mood and opinions in the financial community, AI systems will have the option to anticipate possible market movements and assess sentiment-driven risks.

AI-powered chatbots and virtual assistants are widely used in the financial industry to provide instant responses to customer queries. These virtual assistants handle routine inquiries, assist with account information, and guide customers through basic transactions.

By employing machine learning algorithms, these virtual assistants learn from customer interactions to personalize responses based on individual preferences, transaction history, and frequently asked questions.

AI-driven robo-advisors offer personalized investment advice based on customer financial goals, risk tolerance, and market conditions. These platforms use algorithms to create and manage investment portfolios tailored to each customer's unique profile. Machine learning models continuously analyze customer behavior, preferences, and market trends to refine and personalize investment recommendations over time.

Voice assistants and biometric authentication methods, such as voice recognition and fingerprint scans, provide secure and convenient access to financial services. AI algorithms verify user identities, reducing the risk of unauthorized access.

Voice assistants will be programmed to recognize individual voices and preferences, providing a personalized experience for users. This personalization enhances customer satisfaction and loyalty.

AI-driven predictive analytics analyze customer data to anticipate their needs. By assessing transaction history, spending patterns, and life events, financial institutions can proactively offer relevant products and services. Recommendations based on predictive analytics are highly personalized, leading to a more tailored customer experience and increased engagement.

AI algorithms are crucial for real-time fraud detection. By analyzing transaction patterns, user behavior, and other data points, AI systems identify and flag potentially fraudulent activities.

AI contributes to personalization by recognizing normal spending patterns and behaviors for each customer, allowing it to identify deviations that may indicate fraudulent transactions.

AI streamlines customer support workflows by automating routine tasks, such as account inquiries, transaction history requests, and basic problem resolution. This improves response times and operational efficiency. AI-driven automation will be personalized by incorporating customer data, ensuring that responses are contextually relevant and tailored to individual customer needs.

AI analytics tools analyze customer interactions across various channels, including websites, mobile apps, and social media. Thus financial institutions understand customer behavior and preferences.

• • • •

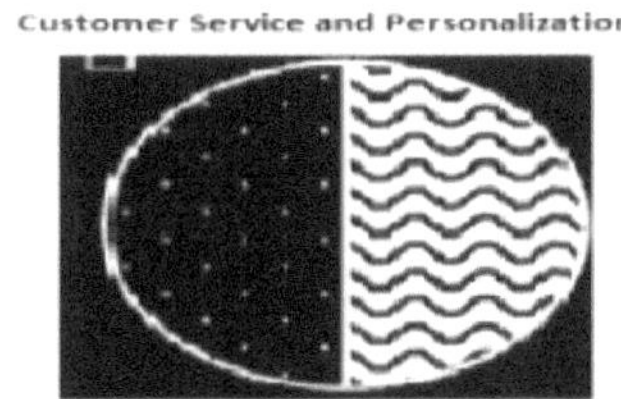

• • • •

By gaining insights from customer engagement data, financial institutions personalize marketing messages, offers, and product recommendations, enhancing the overall customer experience.

AI facilitates omni-channel personalization, ensuring a consistent customer experience across different channels (online, mobile, branch). Customer preferences and interactions are seamlessly integrated for a unified and personalized experience. Consistent personalization contributes to increased customer satisfaction and loyalty as customers receive a cohesive and tailored experience regardless of the channel they use.

• • • •

Credit Scoring and Lending.

• • • •

AI facilitates for more nuanced and accurate credit scoring, enabling financial institutions to make better lending decisions, especially for individuals with limited credit histories. Fairness and transparency in AI-driven lending decisions are crucial to prevent discrimination.

Traditional credit scoring models may be limited in assessing the creditworthiness of individuals with thin credit files or those who lack a traditional banking history. AI algorithms examine with precision alternative data sources, such as social media activity, online behavior, and even smartphone usage patterns to build more comprehensive risk profiles. This results in greater clarity for financial institutions make more informed lending decisions and manage credit risk effectively.

* * * *

Types of Data Used for Credit Scoring

Examples of factors are as follows:

- Payment history: A record of late payments on current and past credit accounts may have an adverse effect on an individual's score. Payments on time and in full may improve the score.
- Public records: Matters of public record such as bankruptcies, judgments, and collection items may impact the score.
- Amount owed and loan purpose: High levels of debt may impact the score. The purpose of the loan and the type of CSP may also be linked to creditworthiness.
- Length of credit history and length of time at address: Length of credit history and time at current address are associated with creditworthiness.
- New accounts: Opening multiple new credit accounts in a short period of time may impact the score.
- Credit bureau checks: Whenever a request for a credit report is made, the inquiry is recorded. Recent inquiries may impact the score.
- Social media data: Social media data may provide insights into a consumer's lifestyle, indicating creditworthiness.
- Mobile data: Mobile data may provide granular information and insights into consumer behavior.
- Utilities data: A steady record of payments may contribute to an individual's credit score.
- Commercial data: Financial statements, operational information, and working capital loans may indicate the creditworthiness of businesses.
- Macroeconomic data: A change in the macroeconomy (that is, a change in the unemployment rate or GDP of a region) may impact the credit scores of consumers and businesses in that region.

* * * *

Traditional credit scoring models primarily rely on historical credit data from credit bureaus to assess an individual's creditworthiness. This approach may be inadequate for individuals with thin credit files or those who lack a traditional banking history, such as young adults or recent immigrants.

Example: A recent college graduate who has just started working may have limited credit history because they have not yet taken out loans or held credit cards. Traditional credit scoring models might struggle to provide an accurate assessment of their creditworthiness due to the lack of sufficient historical credit data.

AI algorithms review alternative data sources beyond traditional credit data. These alternative sources include social media activity, online behavior, and smartphone usage patterns. By considering a broader set of data points, AI algorithms build more nuanced and comprehensive risk profiles.

More examples:

AI algorithms perform inspections about social media profiles to assess an individual's online presence, connections, and reputation. For example, responsible financial behavior could be inferred from positive online interactions and community engagement.

Examining online shopping patterns, payment histories for digital services, or the types of websites visited provide insights into financial habits that traditional credit scoring models might miss.

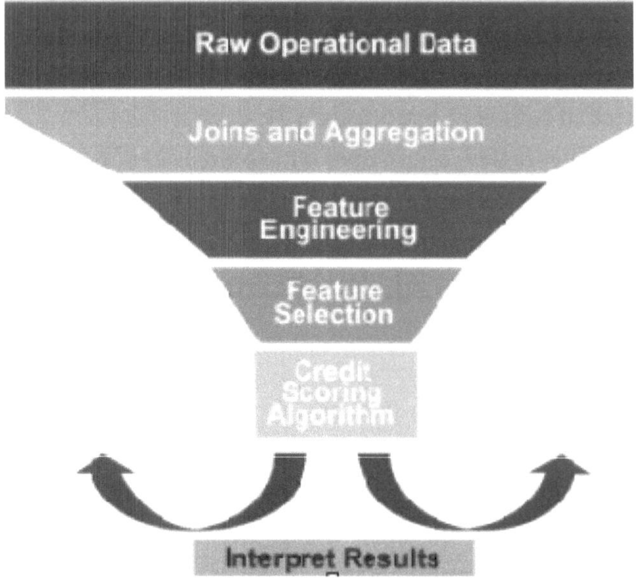

AI algorithms analyze perform smartphone data, such as app usage, location data, and communication patterns, to gain a better understanding of an individual's lifestyle and financial behavior. For instance, regular bill payments through mobile banking apps might indicate financial responsibility.

By incorporating insights from alternative data sources, AI algorithms build more comprehensive risk profiles for individuals. This clarifies to financial institutions to make more informed lending decisions and better manage credit risk, especially for those who may not have a well-established credit history.

Example: consider a freelancer or gig economy worker who may not have a stable income documented in traditional credit reports. AI algorithms inspect their digital footprint, including income patterns from freelance platforms, online financial transactions, and social media endorsements, to assess their creditworthiness more accurately.

• • • •

Regulatory Compliance.

• • • •

AI automate compliance processes, ensuring financial institutions adhere to complex and evolving regulations. The rapid evolution of AI technology may outpace regulatory frameworks, leading to challenges in maintaining compliance. Striking a balance between innovation and regulation is essential.

Examples: IBM OpenPages, SAS Risk Management. These platforms incorporate AI capabilities to automate regulatory compliance processes, such as AML and KYC, ensuring that financial institutions comply with current regulations.

IBM OpenPages is an integrated governance, risk, and compliance (GRC) platform designed to help organizations manage risk and compliance activities effectively. It provides a centralized system for risk assessment, policy management, regulatory compliance, and reporting.

IBM OpenPages incorporates AI and advanced analytics to enhance its capabilities. In the context of regulatory compliance, the platform uses AI for:

- AI algorithms analyze large volumes of data, including transaction records, customer information, and external data sources, to identify patterns indicative of potential money laundering activities.

- The platform employs machine learning models to assess and prioritize risks. This includes identifying high-risk transactions or customers, ensuring that the organization focuses its resources on mitigating the most significant compliance risks.

- AI-powered monitoring enables real-time detection of anomalies and suspicious activities, contributing to proactive compliance management.

- IBM OpenPages facilitates AML and KYC compliance by automating key processes:

- The platform automates the collection and analysis of customer information, streamlining the KYC process. AI verify identities and assess about the risk associated with each customer (Customer Due Diligence -CDD).

- AI algorithms continuously monitor financial transactions for unusual patterns, enabling the detection of potentially suspicious activities; (this is essential for meeting AML regulations that require robust transaction monitoring systems).

SAS Risk Management is a comprehensive solution that enables organizations to identify, assess, and mitigate various types of risks. It covers credit risk, market risk, operational risk, and regulatory compliance, among other risk categories.

SAS Risk Management leverages AI and advanced analytics to provide a holistic approach to risk management. Specifically, in the domain of regulatory compliance, SAS Risk Management uses AI for:

- Machine learning models predict potential risks and identify emerging patterns that may have compliance implications. This proactive approach helps organizations address compliance challenges before they escalate.

- AI-driven behavioral analysis helps in assessing and understanding patterns of transactions and customer behavior. This aids in detecting anomalies and potential fraud, contributing to AML and KYC compliance efforts.

- AI streamlines the process of regulatory reporting by automating data collection and analysis, ensuring that the organization meets reporting requirements accurately and in a timely manner.

- SAS Risk Management supports AML and KYC compliance through:

Organizations will be entitled to benefit from this platform by to define and run scenarios that simulate potential money laundering or fraudulent activities. AI assists in analyzing the outcomes and providing insights to strengthen compliance measures. AI-driven customer risk profiling helps in categorizing customers based on their risk levels. This aids in prioritizing KYC efforts and allocating resources more efficiently.

• • • •

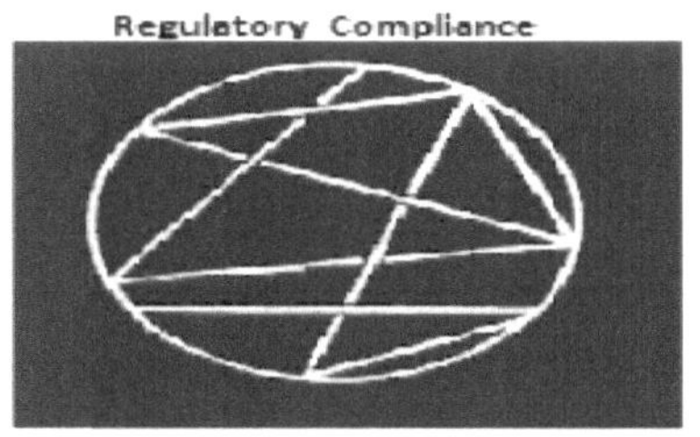

• • • •

Data Security and Privacy.

• • • •

AI strengthen cybersecurity by identifying and responding to potential threats in real-time, enhancing the overall security of financial systems. The collection and use of vast amounts of financial data raise concerns about privacy and the potential for misuse. It highlights the importance of robust data protection measures and ethical data practices.

Behavioral biometrics involves analyzing unique patterns in user behavior, such as typing speed, mouse movements, and touchscreen interactions. In the context of risk management, AI systems use these biometric markers to create a digital fingerprint for users. If a transaction or login attempt deviates significantly from the established behavioral patterns, it could be flagged as a potential security risk, prompting additional authentication measures.

• • • •

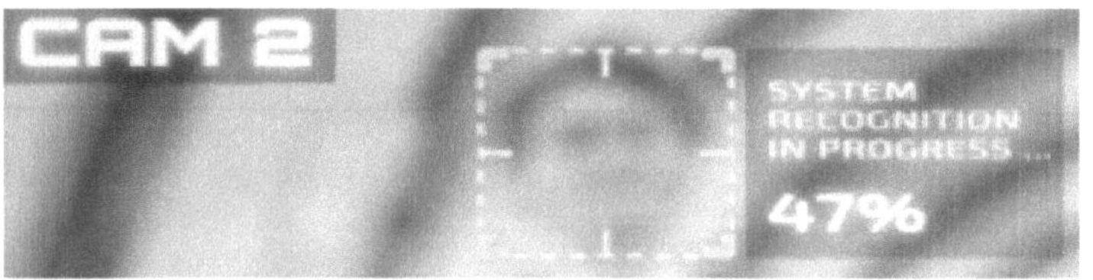

• • • •

AI-driven cybersecurity systems continuously monitor network traffic, user behavior, and system activities to detect potential cyber threats. Machine learning algorithms identify anomalies indicative of a cyber attack, such as unauthorized access attempts, unusual data transfers, or patterns consistent with malware activity.

Blockchain technology, combined with AI, enhance transparency and security in financial transactions. Smart contracts, powered by AI, automatically execute and enforce contractual agreements, reducing the risk of fraud or manipulation in transactions. Additionally, the decentralized nature of blockchain provides a tamper-resistant record of transactions.

Examples: Okta, ForgeRock, Microsoft Azure Active Directory. These systems employ artificial intelligence functions to analyse access patterns and user behaviour, improving security and detecting suspicious activity.

Ethereum, Hyperledger Fabric. These systems provide a secure and decentralised infrastructure for transactions and smart contracts, which improve transparency and security in financial transactions.

• • • •

• • • •

Empowering Ecommerce with Artificial Intelligence: A Symbiotic Relationship.

• • • •

AI algorithms makes screenings of customer data to deliver highly personalized shopping experiences. This includes product recommendations based on browsing and purchase history, personalized email marketing, and dynamic pricing strategies. AI-driven recommendation engines, such as those used by Amazon, analyze user behavior and preferences to suggest products that are more likely to convert.

AI-powered chatbots enhance customer support by providing immediate responses to queries, order tracking, and troubleshooting. These chatbots handle a multitude of customer inquiries simultaneously, ensuring swift and efficient service. Chatbots are available round the clock, offering assistance even when agents are offline.

AI makes its distinctive contribution in the aspect to optimize inventory levels by forecasting demand patterns, identifying slow-moving items, and automating restocking processes. This prevents overstocking and understocking, leading to cost savings and improved customer satisfaction.

AI algorithms analyze historical sales data, seasonality, and external factors to predict future demand accurately.

Visual search technology gives the potential for the customers to search for products using images or photos. This simplifies the shopping process and enhances the user experience. Customers take a picture of an item they like and find similar products in the ecommerce store.

AI algorithms continuously adjust prices based on supply, demand, competitor pricing, and other factors. Dynamic pricing addresses ecommerce businesses remain competitive while maximizing profits. AI monitors competitor prices and suggests pricing strategies to maintain competitiveness.

AI-driven voice assistants like Siri, Google Assistant, and Alexa facilitate voice commerce by enabling users to place orders and make purchases through voice commands. This represents a growing frontier in ecommerce. Voice commerce provides a hands-free shopping experience, which is particularly convenient for multitasking customers.

AI employs predictive analytics to anticipate customer behavior, enabling businesses to tailor their marketing strategies. It target high-value customers, forecast future sales, and optimize advertising campaigns. Predictive analytics informs the timing and content of marketing campaigns to maximize their impact.

Predictive models help make weather forecasts, develop video games, translate voice-to-text messages, customer service decisions, and develop investment portfolios. Types of predictive models include decision trees, regression, and neural networks.

2.2. AI-Driven Business Strategies

Business strategies encompass a wide range of approaches and plans that organizations develop and implement to achieve their goals and objectives. In the dynamic landscape of today's global markets, the formulation of effective business strategies is essential for maintaining a competitive edge and navigating the complexities of the business environment.

These strategies serve as roadmaps, guiding organizations in allocating resources, making informed decisions, and responding to ever-changing market conditions. From establishing a market presence and optimizing operational efficiency to fostering innovation and adapting to emerging trends, the formulation and execution of business strategies are central to an organization's ability to thrive and prosper in the face of challenges and opportunities.

In the context of AI-driven strategies, innovation becomes a key focal point. Organizations are increasingly incorporating AI into their research and development processes, exploring new avenues for product and service enhancement. The strategic integration of AI is not merely about technology adoption but also about fostering a culture of continuous improvement and exploration.

Furthermore, ethical considerations and responsible AI use are integral components of modern business strategies. As organizations deploy AI systems, there is a growing emphasis on ensuring transparency, fairness, and accountability. Aligning AI strategies with ethical principles not only safeguards against potential risks but also builds trust among stakeholders, customers, and the broader community.

AI-Powered Market Expansion Strategy.

• • • •

In the era of Artificial Intelligence (AI), businesses are revolutionizing market expansion strategies by harnessing the capabilities of advanced technologies. Consider a retail company that, equipped with AI-driven market analysis, identifies optimal international locations for opening stores.

Through predictive modeling and data-driven insights, the company tailor its offerings to specific demographics, ensuring a seamless expansion into diverse markets.

AI not only facilitates the identification of promising regions but also aids in understanding local consumer behaviors, preferences, and market trends. This approach to market expansion leverages the power of AI to make informed decisions, fostering global growth while optimizing resource allocation and minimizing risks.

AI is changing digital marketing in several ways, bringing significant advancements to the industry.

AI-enhanced marketing automation can gather, organise, analyse, and segment valuable marketing data from multiple sources. This automation not only saves time, but also improves data accuracy and accessibility, providing marketers with a centralised location for data storage and utilisation in marketing campaigns.

AI algorithms enable faster and more comprehensive A/B testing. From web copy to design elements, AI run campaigns through algorithms, learning and improving with each iteration. This enhances the efficiency of testing and provides marketers with more insightful results to optimise their marketing strategies.

AI-powered virtual assistants, such as chatbots, offer around-the-clock customer support. These virtual agents leverage user data to inform sales and advertising efforts, freeing up human agents for more complex tasks. They enhance the customer experience by providing self-serve ways for consumers to find information and make informed purchasing decisions.

AI utilises big data to build robust profiles for leads, cross-referencing social media trends, web interactions, and public records. This enables targeted lead generation and personalised marketing messages, predicting conversion likelihood and executing follow-up actions, thus optimising lead qualification and nurturing.

AI-powered natural language processing and machine learning enable the creation of marketing content and interpretation of user reactions. While AI cannot replicate the creativity of human writers, it generate personalised content suggestions, ad copy, subject headlines, and calls to action, augmenting the content creation process.

• • • •

AI-Enhanced Product Diversification Strategy.

• • • •

A technology company that initially specialized in laptops but, driven by AI insights, identifies opportunities to diversify into smartphones and tablets. AI algorithms analyze market demands, competitor landscapes, and emerging trends to inform strategic decisions on product expansion.

This data-driven approach ensures that the company not only introduces new products but does so with a deep understanding of evolving consumer needs. Through AI-enhanced product diversification, organizations mitigate risks associated with over-reliance on a single product line, staying agile and responsive to the dynamic technology market.

The integration of AI transforms product diversification into a strategic, data-informed initiative, contributing to sustained business growth and competitiveness.

AI systems are capable of making statistical predictions, which means inferring diagnosis and analysis based on the information previously obtained, while sifting through big data and adjusting their algorithms. The use of advanced statistical techniques for deriving prediction is commonly referred to as predictive analytics, which is a subset area of data analytics.

For instance, AI increase efficiency in asset maintenance and management. Predictive maintenance enables identification of when and where an asset is likely to malfunction, and repairing of its parts before they break down.

Information on the condition of assets is collected in real-time through IoT sensors, which are combined with historical life cycle data to diagnose the status of assets and detect anomalies.

Compared to reactive maintenance, predictive maintenance presents substantial benefits by reducing downtime (or risks of), and subsequently reducing cost of production or business interruption in case of incident, while avoiding unnecessary routine maintenance.

• • • •

AI-Driven Cost Leadership Strategy.

• • • •

Picture an airline that harnesses AI for comprehensive cost management. Through predictive analytics, machine learning algorithms analyze historical data and real-time variables to optimize fuel consumption, strategically schedule maintenance, and fine-tune crew schedules, thereby significantly reducing operational costs.

AI-driven route optimization considers dynamic factors like weather patterns and air traffic, ensuring not only cost savings but also enhanced operational reliability. This fusion of AI and cost leadership not only enables the airline to offer competitive ticket prices but also fortifies its position as an industry leader, illustrating how technological innovation becomes integral to achieving sustainable cost advantages.

The example of an airline underscores how AI, through continuous learning from data, empowers businesses to identify and implement cost-saving measures dynamically. AI-driven cost leadership goes beyond traditional approaches, enabling real-time adjustments and proactive decision-making.

The strategic integration of AI in cost leadership strategies ensures that organizations not only reduce operational expenses but also stay ahead in a rapidly evolving business landscape. By embracing AI, companies establish themselves as efficient and cost-effective industry players, driving competitive pricing, increasing market share, and fostering long-term sustainability.

• • • •

AI-Infused Differentiation Strategy.

• • • •

Take, for instance, a luxury automobile manufacturer that intertwines AI with its differentiation strategy. Through machine learning algorithms, the manufacturer tailors vehicle designs based on real-time consumer preferences, historical market trends, and emerging styles.

AI-enhanced design processes ensure that each car reflects not only superior craftsmanship but also aligns with the evolving tastes of discerning consumers. Moreover, the integration of advanced technology, such as AI-driven autonomous features and cutting-edge infotainment systems, adds an extra layer of distinctiveness, positioning the brand as a pioneer in innovation.

This symbiosis of AI and differentiation not only creates a line of cars perceived as unique but also establishes the manufacturer as a trailblazer in delivering unparalleled automotive excellence.

The example of a luxury automobile manufacturer showcases how AI, through its capacity to analyze vast datasets, enhances the understanding of consumer preferences and market dynamics. AI algorithms continually learn from user feedback, market trends, and even social media sentiments to refine and customize the differentiation strategy.

By incorporating AI-driven innovation, organizations create products that not only meet but exceed evolving consumer expectations. This strategic fusion allows businesses not only to command premium prices but also to stay at the forefront of market trends, demonstrating that AI is not just a tool but a catalyst for sustained differentiation and brand eminence.

By aligning brand strategy with AI-driven analytics, businesses can gain a deep understanding of their customers, identify emerging trends, and make data-backed strategic decisions that enhance their brand's position in the market.

In the age of AI, brand strategy emerges as a powerful tool for businesses seeking to navigate the evolving landscape successfully. It enables businesses to humanize the AI experience, differentiate themselves, foster trust, and maintain authenticity in a highly automated world.

By integrating brand strategy with AI technologies, businesses can create meaningful connections, build customer loyalty, and establish a distinct competitive advantage. Embrace the power of brand strategy in the age of AI, and unlock the immense potential to thrive in this new era of automation.

• • • •

AI-Integrated Digital Transformation Strategy.

• • • •

Consider a traditional brick-and-mortar retailer navigating the digital landscape by incorporating AI into its transformation strategy. Through advanced data analytics powered by AI algorithms, the retailer gains deep insights into consumer preferences, buying patterns, and market trends.

AI-driven personalization enhances the online shopping experience, tailoring recommendations and promotions based on individual customer behaviors. Additionally, machine learning algorithms optimize inventory management, predicting demand fluctuations and ensuring efficient supply chain operations.

By strategically leveraging e-commerce platforms, mobile apps, and AI-driven analytics, the retailer not only adapts to evolving consumer behaviors but also positions itself as an agile and technologically advanced player in the digital marketplace.

The example of a brick-and-mortar retailer underscores how AI augments digital initiatives by providing actionable insights and enhancing operational efficiency. AI algorithms, continuously learning from user interactions, enable the retailer to offer personalized experiences that resonate with individual preferences.

Moreover, AI contributes to the optimization of internal processes, making them more adaptive and responsive to market dynamics. The strategic fusion of digital transformation and AI not only propels businesses into the digital age but also positions them to harness the full potential of emerging technologies.

It's not merely a shift to digital; it's a paradigm where AI becomes the driving force behind enhanced customer experiences, streamlined operations, and a competitive edge in the ever-evolving digital landscape.

• • • •

AI-Enhanced Market Segmentation Strategy.

• • • • •

Imagine an electronics company that not only identifies consumer segments but also utilizes AI to dynamically adapt its marketing campaigns in real-time. Through predictive modeling, AI algorithms examines vast datasets, identifying patterns and preferences within each segment.

This enables the company to tailor not only its marketing messages but also product features and pricing to resonate with the unique needs and expectations of tech enthusiasts, budget-conscious buyers, and professionals.

The application of AI in market segmentation ensures a level of precision and responsiveness that goes beyond traditional approaches, allowing the electronics company to establish stronger connections with diverse consumer segments and maximize the effectiveness of its marketing efforts.

In the context of the electronics company, AI algorithms continuously learn from customer interactions, refining segmentation models and adapting strategies based on evolving consumer behaviors. The dynamic nature of AI-driven market segmentation makes it possible for the company to respond swiftly to emerging trends and shifts in consumer preferences.

Moreover, AI facilitates the identification of previously unseen patterns, ensuring that the company remains proactive in reaching niche markets and uncovering new opportunities. By embracing AI in market segmentation, organizations not only enhance their precision in targeting specific demographics but also foster a more agile and adaptive approach to marketing that aligns seamlessly with the ever-changing landscape of consumer preferences.

We can think of AI as a component of algorithms that use a non-linear approach to gather millions of data points (Big Data) and synthesize it into useful insights for our marketing.

With AI we can marry unlimited customer variables into the algorithms in real time, and find the optimal segmentation among these. This approach links the segmentation to business results that is embedded into the code. When we connect all our data and apply AI to it, we create:

• A 360 degree view of the customer and data input in real time and constantly updated in real time so that we know what our customers are responding to and you can adjust your marketing accordingly. We won't have siloed data that lacks integration.

• Effective segmentation treats each customer as an individual based on their individual needs. We know the "one size fits all" approach doesn't work. AI can help you hone in on preferred channels and messaging to connect with individuals.

• Identify inconsistencies in behaviour to spark serious personalization. Marketers who develop well-optimized strategies that align your marketing tactics with customer behaviours have the opportunity to create more personal connections with our customers.

In the era of personalization, that's a very real competitive advantage. We will be able to work with our clients to create a powerful combination of business strategy with customized algorithms that incorporate all your data (CRM, CMS, social media) in one platform and deliver the information we need to develop a successful marketing strategy. As a marketer, we want to trim costs and increase revenue. Applying AI to our customer segmentation can help us optimize our marketing channels.

• • • •

AI-Driven Mergers and Acquisitions (M&A) Strategy.

• • • •

Envision a pharmaceutical company that, fueled by AI insights, acquires a smaller biotech firm to access its cutting-edge drug pipeline. AI algorithms play a pivotal role in the due diligence process, analyzing vast datasets related to the biotech firm's research, development methodologies, and potential market impact.

This data-driven approach not only facilitates informed decision-making gives the pharmaceutical company the option to seamlessly integrate the innovative capabilities of the acquired firm into its own research and development initiatives.

By strategically leveraging AI in M&A, the pharmaceutical company not only accelerates its growth trajectory but also fortifies its position as a leader in pharmaceutical innovation, illustrating how technology becomes a catalyst for strategic expansion and industry leadership.

In the scenario of the pharmaceutical company, AI algorithms continually learn from the integrated data streams of both entities, optimizing research and development processes. The predictive capabilities of AI also contribute to identifying potential areas of synergy, ensuring a harmonious integration that maximizes the benefits of the acquisition.

Moreover, AI aids in assessing market dynamics, potential risks, and growth opportunities, enabling the pharmaceutical company to navigate the complexities of the pharmaceutical landscape with agility.

The strategic fusion of AI and M&A not only facilitates the identification of strategic targets but also ensures a seamless assimilation of capabilities, positioning organizations for sustained growth and innovation in an ever-evolving industry.

Furthermore, AI-powered analytics unlock hidden insights that can enhance post-merger activities. These analytics identify cross-selling opportunities, optimize supply chains, and enhance operational efficiencies. Predictive models built on AI algorithms enable organizations to anticipate potential challenges and develop proactive mitigation strategies.

Additionally, AI support talent retention efforts by identifying key employees critical to the success of the integrated entity, thus enabling effective workforce management during the integration process.

Another concern is the transparency and interpretability of AI algorithms. Some AI models, such as deep learning neural networks, are highly complex and challenging to interpret.

The lack of transparency in AI decision-making raise regulatory and ethical concerns, particularly when dealing with sensitive information. Organizations must establish clear governance frameworks and ensure compliance with legal and ethical standards when using AI in the M&A process.

• • • •

AI-Infused Sustainability and Corporate Responsibility Strategy.

• • • •

An energy company that, propelled by AI insights, commits to an ambitious agenda of reducing carbon emissions and increasing energy efficiency. AI algorithms play a crucial role in monitoring and optimizing energy consumption, identifying areas for improvement, and predicting potential environmental impacts.

Additionally, AI-driven analytics contribute to the identification of renewable energy opportunities and the development of innovative solutions to address sustainability challenges.

By strategically integrating AI into its sustainability efforts, the energy company aligns with ethical and regulatory expectations and pioneers data-driven approaches to mitigating its ecological footprint, showcasing how technology becomes a driving force for responsible and sustainable corporate practices.

Integrating AI into sustainability and corporate responsibility strategies provides organizations with unprecedented insights into their ESG performance, fostering a holistic and proactive approach.

In the case of the energy company, AI continuously learns from environmental data, helping optimize resource usage and minimize ecological impact.

The predictive capabilities of AI aid in anticipating future sustainability challenges, allowing the company to proactively address issues and stay ahead of regulatory requirements. Moreover, AI facilitates transparent reporting and communication of sustainability initiatives to stakeholders, building trust and demonstrating a commitment to responsible business practices.

The strategic fusion of AI and sustainability shapes organizations with global sustainability goals and positions them as leaders in incorporating technology to address complex environmental and social challenges.

According to several research studies, 80% of business leaders reported that their sustainability programs help to reduce their organization's costs. Embedding sustainability in an organization's strategy can play a crucial role in cost reduction, improving supply chains, and fostering organizational adaptability in the face of disruptions.

Investments in technologies like data analytics and cloud computing have helped organizations measure and quantify their carbon impact and identify areas for improvement, and efficiencies.

• • • •

AI-Driven Customer-Centric Strategy.

• • • •

Visualize an online retailer that, guided by AI insights, goes beyond conventional approaches to invest in cutting-edge personalization. Through machine learning algorithms, the retailer analyzes customer behaviors, preferences, and historical interactions to tailor product recommendations with unparalleled accuracy.

AI-driven chatbots and virtual assistants enhance customer support by providing real-time, context-aware assistance, ensuring swift issue resolution. Loyalty programs benefit from predictive analytics, which identify personalized incentives and rewards that resonate with individual customers.

By strategically integrating AI into its customer-centric approach, the online retailer not only meets customer expectations but anticipates needs, fostering a deeper level of engagement and loyalty, illustrating how technology becomes a catalyst for building enduring customer relationships.

AI algorithms continually learn from customer interactions across various touchpoints, refining the understanding of individual preferences. Predictive analytics help forecast future customer needs, allowing the retailer to proactively adapt its offerings and services.

Moreover, AI contributes to the enhancement of feedback mechanisms, ensuring that customer insights are leveraged to refine and optimize the overall customer experience continuously.

The strategic fusion of AI and customer-centricity positions organizations as leaders in customer experience and demonstrates a commitment to leveraging technology for the benefit of the customer, showcasing the transformative impact of AI on building lasting and meaningful customer relationships.

We could talk about a five-point strategy:

1. Deep Customer Research: dive into the heart of what our customers truly desire. Adopt both qualitative and quantitative research tools—surveys, focus groups, interviews, and real-time feedback.

This step ensures we are building our strategy on solid ground. Instead of making assumptions, we are drawing from genuine customer sentiments, laying down the cornerstone for a strategy that genuinely aligns customer value, with your customers' aspirations and requirements.

2. Customer Journey Mapping: imagine walking in our customer's shoes. That's precisely what customer journey mapping achieves. It traces the entire arc of a customer's interaction with our brand—from the first inkling of awareness to the post-purchase phase.

By charting out this journey, we can identify key touchpoints, unearth potential challenges, and spot opportunities to delight our customers. In essence, it's about ensuring every twist and turn in the journey is smooth and memorable.

3. Institutionalize Customer Feedback: a strategy that doesn't evolve is one that stagnates. Setting up systematic channels for feedback—be it monthly surveys, quarterly check-ins, or annual NPS evaluations—ensures us always have our ear to the ground.

But gathering feedback isn't enough; acting on it is crucial. By continually iterating based on what our customers tell us, we send a powerful message—that their voice matters, and we are here to serve them better, every single day.

4. Employee Training and Empowerment: our employees are the custodians of the customer centric brand and experience. Equip them with the knowledge and tools to champion customer centricity.

By instilling in them the significance of a customer-first mindset and giving them the autonomy and resources to make customer-centric decisions, we ensure that every interaction our customer has with our brand is consistent, positive, and value-driven.

5. Leverage Technology and Data Analytics: in the digital age, understanding customer behavior goes beyond just feedback. Employ advanced data analytics tools to glean insights from customer interactions across digital platforms.

This not only helps in personalizing experiences but also in anticipating customer needs, even before the customer vocalizes them. Technology, when wielded correctly, can be the magic wand that transforms a business's customer-centric aspirations into tangible outcomes.

• • • •

AI-Infused Innovation and R&D Strategy.

• • • •

Envision a technology company that, guided by AI insights, not only allocates a significant budget to R&D but strategically integrates AI into every facet of the innovation process. AI-driven predictive modeling analyzes vast datasets, identifying emerging trends, consumer preferences, and potential areas for disruptive innovation.

This data-driven approach not only streamlines the identification of research priorities but also enhances the efficiency of the R&D process. Machine learning algorithms continuously learn from experimentation outcomes, refining hypotheses and guiding researchers toward more promising avenues.

By embracing AI in its innovation and R&D endeavors, the technology company not only sustains its commitment to cutting-edge advancements but also accelerates the pace of discovery, showcasing how technology becomes a driving force for sustained innovation and competitive excellence.

In the example of the technology company, AI algorithms continually learn from the evolving tech landscape, providing real-time intelligence on emerging technologies and market dynamics.

Predictive analytics aid in identifying high-potential innovation areas, guiding the allocation of resources for maximum impact. Additionally, AI contributes to optimizing the testing and prototyping phases, ensuring that R&D efforts are focused on initiatives with the highest likelihood of success.

The strategic fusion of AI and innovation enhances the effectiveness of R&D processes and ranks organizations as leaders in driving industry advancements, highlighting the pivotal role of AI in shaping the future landscape of technology and innovation.

• • • •

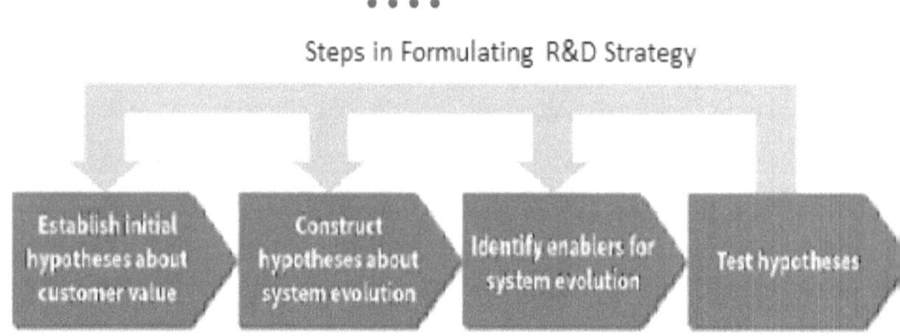

• • • •

Figure shows the steps involved in formulating this R&D strategy. Rather than pursuing trends in technology as such, it is necessary to start by asking what type of customer value is desirable and in which cases should it be created.

Once hypotheses for customer value are established, the next step is to construct hypotheses for the system evolution needed to achieve this value. The term "system" is used here not only in the sense of artifacts built from a combination of computers and machinery, but also in the sense of a so-called business ecosystem(3), (4).

That is, it is made up of three layers: the mechanisms used to create value, the artifacts that make this possible, and the agents that provide these artifacts. Once the hypotheses for system evolution are constructed, the next step is to determine the specific technologies for AI and analytics that will serve as the enablers for the artifacts in the second layer.

Of course, systems require more than just technology. The construction of a sustainable ecosystem also needs to consider things like economics, rule-making, and how to involve customers and partners.

2.3. Software Approaches and Interactions

The Options of choosing Workday.

. . . .

Workday is a prominent cloud-based human resources (HR) and financial management software system designed for the improvement and manage various aspects of organizations workforce and financial operations, including a range of solutions for human resources, finance, and payroll management.

Workday offers a comprehensive suite of HR solutions, including employee data management, payroll processing, benefits administration, and talent management. It helps organizations streamline HR processes and improve workforce management.

Workday provides financial management tools that cover accounting, financial reporting, procurement, and expenses. It aims to simplify financial operations and reporting for businesses and is a cloud-based software platform, which means it is hosted and accessed via the internet. This increases scalability, accessibility, and reduced dependence on on-premises infrastructure.

Workday is known for its user-friendly and intuitive interface, making it easier for employees and administrators to navigate and use the software. The program offers integration capabilities, enabling it to connect with other software systems and tools that an organization may use, such as third-party HR applications or financial software. Workday provides analytics and reporting tools that help organizations gain insights into their workforce and financial data, enabling data-driven decision-making.

. . . .

Security is a significant concern for HR and financial data. Workday incorporates robust security measures to protect sensitive information and ensure compliance with data privacy regulations. Workday offers mobile apps, users have the chance to access HR and financial information from smartphones and tablets, promoting flexibility and remote work capabilities.

When it comes to financial management, Workday provides various tools and features to help organizations effectively manage their finances, offering a comprehensive suite of financial tools to meet the needs of businesses of various sizes and industries.

One key aspect of financial management is tracking and managing expenses. Organizations can through Workday to streamline their expense tracking processes. Employees use Workday to submit their expense reports electronically.

They input details such as receipts, expense categories, and project codes. Workday's financial management module is configured to have an approval workflow. Supervisors or managers review and approve expense reports directly within the system.

• • • •

• • • •

Can enforce expense policies and rules, ensuring that expenses comply with company guidelines and are within budgetary limits. Finance teams access real-time data on expenses, having the possibility to monitor spending patterns and identify areas where cost savings will be achieved.

Workday provides robust reporting and analytics tools that offers facilities for organizations to generate various financial reports. For example, they create expense trend reports, budget vs. actual reports, and detailed breakdowns of expenses by category, department, or project.

Can integrate with other financial systems and third-party applications, making it easier to consolidate financial data and streamline processes. By using Workday's financial management capabilities for expense tracking and reporting, organizations achieve greater control over their finances, reduce manual data entry, enforce compliance, and gain insights into their spending patterns.

Workday is well-known for its HR and Payroll Management capabilities. Might be fitted with options for HR and Payroll Management, Employee Onboarding and Payroll Processing.

Workday provides a streamlined onboarding process. When a new employee is hired, their information is entered into the system. This include personal details, employment contracts, tax forms, and more. The system also initiate background checks and other pre-employment processes.

Workday's payroll module permits organizations to configure payroll rules, tax codes, and payment frequencies. This setup ensures that employees are paid accurately and on time. Has the option to integrate with time and attendance systems or offer its own time tracking features. Employees log their hours worked, request time off, and supervisors can approve these requests within the platform.

• • • •

Streamline expense processes
- Intuitive web based self-service application.
- Configurable approval processes.
- Automatic credit card transaction loads.
- Configurable instruction text.
- Reinbursement by direct deposit.
- Ability to delegate expense report creation or approvals.
- Reinbursement accounts.
- Fast settlements.

Spend controls and management
- Applicant and contingent about expenses.
- Expense reports on behalf of external committee members.
- Transaction approval and audit history.
- Policy compliance audit.
- Exception management.
- Spend authorisations.
- Cash advances.
- Spend freezes by organisation.
- Expense item restrictions.
- Eligibilities and deductions.

Can manage employee benefits, including health insurance, retirement plans, and other perks. Employees enroll in benefits during onboarding or during designated open enrollment periods. Workday automates payroll calculations based on the configured rules and employee data. This includes deductions, taxes, and any other adjustments. The system generates paychecks or initiates direct deposits.

Helps ensure tax compliance by calculating and withholding the correct federal, state, and local taxes from employee paychecks. It also generates tax forms such as W-2s for employees at the end of the year.

Offers self-service portals for employees where they access pay stubs, tax documents, and update personal information. This reduces the burden on HR and payroll teams for handling routine inquiries.

Provides robust reporting and analytics tools for HR and payroll data. HR managers and finance teams generate reports on payroll costs, employee turnover, and compliance metrics. May be integrated with other systems such as accounting software for accurate financial reporting and general ledger reconciliation.

• • • •

By providing employees with an intuitive and user-friendly interface, which is designed to be intuitive and easy to navigate, Workday empowers individuals to take control of their HR-related tasks, reduces the burden on HR staff for routine inquiries, and enhances overall user satisfaction with the system.

One of the key aspects of Workday's user-friendly interface is its Employee SelfService Portal. This portal considerably facilitates employees to access and manage their own HR related information and tasks with ease.

When an employee logs into Workday, they are greeted with a personalized dashboard. This dashboard provides a snapshot of important information, such as upcoming tasks, notifications, and reminders. For example, an employee might see reminders for timesheet submission or benefits enrollment.

The menu structure and navigation are designed to be straightforward. Employees easily find the information they need, whether it's related to their personal profile, pay stubs, benefits, or time-off requests. The menu is logically organized, making it easy to locate specific tasks.

Employees view and update their personal information, such as contact details, emergency contacts, and tax withholdings. They also upload documents, such as resumes or certifications. Workday's time tracking and attendance features are designed for simplicity. Employees log their hours worked, request time off, and view their time-off balances. Approving managers quickly review and approve these requests.

Workday Expenses

Reporting and insight

- Approval and exception notifications.
- Embedded analytics during approvals.
- Real time consolidated spend insight.
- drill-down analysis by business dimensions.
- Standard reporting library and custom report writer.
- Expense management dashboard.
- Information export for regulatory reporting.

Global core

- Multi-language support.
- Multi-currency support.
- Global consistency and auditability.
- Ability to upload local travel and reimbursement rates.
- Support for local reimbursement policies.
- Global credit card formats.
- Local vehicle mileage reimbursement rates.
Transaction tax default.
- Value-added tax.

Unified with workday Financial Management and Workday Human Capital Management

- Rapid deployment and adoption.
- Unified login and user experience.
- Single home page for HR and expenses.
- Immediate accounting visibility upon approval.

• • • •

During open enrollment periods, employees easily select and enroll in their benefits through the self-service portal. The system may provide helpful explanations and comparisons of available benefits options. Employees access their pay stubs, view payroll history, and make changes to their direct deposit information. It's easy to understand their earnings, deductions, and taxes.

Workday often includes task assistance features, such as step-by-step wizards and tooltips, to guide employees through various processes. This works ensuring that employees complete tasks accurately. The search functionality is robust, In this way, the employees will quickly find specific information or documents they need. They use natural language search queries to locate relevant content.

Effectively monitor and control spend.
Eliminate manual paper processes and easily configure expense workflows and approvals. We can also implement spend authorisations ans spend freezes to plan for control, or halt spending. Every transaction is recorded for audit transparency and embedded analytics helps inform manager approvals and administrative decisions.

Mobility and ease of use for the workforce.
The easier it is for workers to submit expense reports, the lower the costs, the more accurate the accounting and the more timely the reimbursements. Workday offers an easy-to-use consumer web-like application, as well as an intuitive mobile experience that allows us to submit and approve expenses on the go from any web enabled device.

Workday is known for its robust integration capabilities, that connects organizations to their Workday systems with various third-party applications and services. By integrating with a payroll service provider, organizations benefit from specialized payroll expertise while still leveraging Workday's HR and financial management capabilities.

Many organizations use external payroll service providers to manage their payroll processes. Workday integrate seamlessly with these payroll providers to ensure accurate and efficient payroll processing.

It can be configured for synchronize employee data, such as names, addresses, tax information, and salary details, with the external payroll service provider's system. This ensures that both systems have consistent and up-to-date employee information.

Workday send necessary payroll data to the external provider, including hours worked, overtime, bonuses, and deductions. The payroll provider performs the payroll calculations based on this data.

• • • •

Getting Started with Workday Reports

* Reports are built directly into Workday
* Reports can be accessed through the Search Bar or through your Notifications, if the report runs on a schedule
* Information in reports is generally limited to your department or team but depends on individual reports and security
* Reports can be exported to Excel or PDF files, as needed
* 5 Reports included in today's training – Time Tracking Config – Audit; Timesheet Summary, Time Not Entered; Time Sheet Status; All Work Schedule Calendars

• • • •

It may also perform an integration with tax authorities to calculate and withhold the correct federal, state, and local taxes from employee paychecks. This integration enhances compliance with tax regulations. Information related to direct deposit instructions or check printing be seamlessly transferred from Workday to the payroll service provider, ensuring that employees receive their payments as expected.

Before finalizing payroll, data validation checks are performed to catch any discrepancies or errors between Workday and the payroll provider's system. After processing, payroll reports and summaries will generated and sent back to Workday for record-keeping and reporting purposes.

Employees access their pay stubs and payroll-related information through Workday's self-service portal, even though the payroll processing itself is handled by the external provider. Integrating with a reputable payroll service provider ensures that payroll processing is compliant with relevant labor laws and security standards.

• • • •

Workday Expenses drives customer value

<table>
<tr>
<td>- Lower costs with a unified solution for Workday Financial Management and Workday HCM.

- Automate processes to reduce cycle times.</td>
<td>- Gain insights with access to real data and analytics.
- Improve controls and ensure policy compliance.
- Increase adoption with consumer like internet experience.</td>
</tr>
</table>

Workday offers robust analytics and reporting features that enable organizations to gain insights into their HR and financial data. By leveraging Workday's analytics and reporting tools for turnover analysis, HR departments gain valuable insights into employee retention and attrition patterns. They identify departments or job roles with higher turnover rates, assess the impact of organizational changes or initiatives.

Employee turnover, also known as attrition, is a critical metric for HR departments to monitor and address. Workday's analytics and reporting tools assist HR professionals analyze and understand turnover trends. Workday collects and stores data on employee demographics, employment history, reasons for departure, and other relevant information. This data is regularly updated as employees join, leave, or change positions within the organization.

HR teams create custom metrics and key performance indicators (KPIs) to measure turnover. For example, they define turnover rates by department, job role, location, or time period.

Workday provides pre-built reporting templates specifically designed for turnover analysis. HR professionals use these templates or create custom reports tailored to their organization's needs. Workday offers visualization tools that make it possible for HR teams to create charts, graphs, and interactive dashboards to present turnover data visually, making it easier to identify trends and patterns.

• • • •

> Unified with Workday Human Capital Management
> Workday Expenses is unified with Workday Human Capital Management (HCM) allowing to more quickly and easily deploy Workday Expenses to our workforce.
>
> Unification also allows us to reap all the benefits and features of Workday, including worker profiles, organisation structures business processes and embedded management reporting.

Workday provide benchmarking data, which compares organizations' turnover rates with industry standards or with those of their competitors. This gives HR professionals a better understanding of where they stand relative to their peers. Workday's analytics capabilities also include predictive modeling. HR teams use historical turnover data to predict future attrition trends and take proactive measures to retain key talent.

Workday gives users the option to drill down into the data to investigate the reasons behind turnover. For example, they analyze exit interview data, survey responses, and manager feedback to pinpoint areas for improvement. HR professionals schedule automated reports to be generated regularly (e.g., monthly or quarterly) and distributed to relevant stakeholders, such as HR managers, executives, and department heads.

• • • •

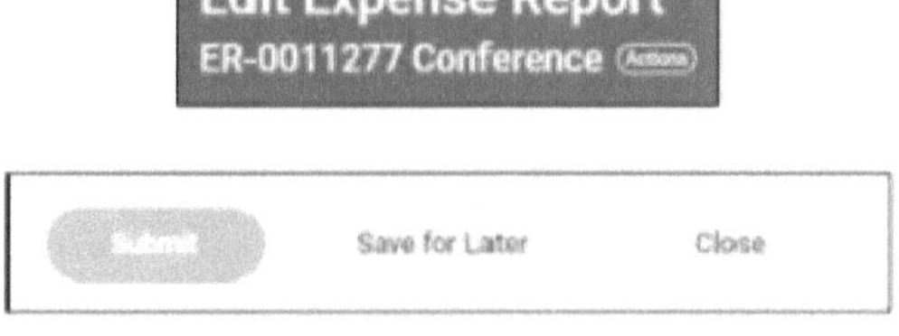

• • • •

Workday places a strong emphasis on security to protect sensitive HR and financial data. By implementing RBAC and other security measures, Workday leads organizations maintain the confidentiality, integrity, and availability of their HR and financial data. These security features ensure that only authorized personnel access and modify sensitive information, reducing the risk of data breaches and unauthorized access.

Role-Based Access Control (RBAC) is a fundamental security feature in Workday that ensures that users have the appropriate level of access based on their roles within the organization. Workday facilitate organizations to define various user roles, such as HR managers, finance analysts, or employees. Each role is associated with specific responsibilities and permissions.

Within each role, organizations configure detailed permissions to specify what actions users in that role can perform. For example, HR managers might have permissions to access and edit employee records, while employees may only have permission to view their own data.

• • • •

• • • •

RBAC extends to data segmentation, meaning that users only access data that is relevant to their roles and responsibilities. For instance, an HR manager for one department won't be able to see sensitive HR information for employees in other departments.

RBAC also applies to workflow approvals. Only users with the appropriate roles and permissions approve certain actions, such as hiring requests, salary adjustments, or expense reports. Workday maintains detailed audit trails of user activity, so organizations are able to track who accessed what data and when, helping to detect and investigate any unauthorized or suspicious activities.

This software enforces strong password policies, including requirements for complex passwords, regular password changes, and account lockout after multiple failed login attempts. Workday supports MFA (Multi-Factor Authentication) to add an extra layer of security.

Users are required to provide a second form of authentication, such as a one-time code from a mobile app, in addition to their password when logging in. Finally, encrypts data both in transit and at rest, ensuring that sensitive information is protected from unauthorized access.

• • • •

How to run a report?.

• • • •

If you want to run a report on Workday, you can search for the report on the search bar. Then click on the report you wanted to run. Based on the report you have chosen, Workday will prompt you to fill in specific reporting criteria like the start date, end date, organization, etc. There are some reports that run without the need for the user to fill in details.

After filling in the details, you can click on ok in order to execute the report. The result is displayed, and it can be filtered using the filter icon that is located in the right corner. You can also export this report in an Excel format by selecting the Excel icon in the filter options.

• • • •

• • • •

Examining Profiles in Workday.

• • • •

The manager and the city/town where he/she works are always displayed on the right. All these options are easily accessible with a simple 'click'. The same as shown in the picture, i.e. phone, email and team. Clicking on 'Team' will display the screen as shown in the image below, showing all the members. Summary' and 'Overview' also appear at the bottom.

Search on the top by Workday ID. Print icon on the right.

In turn, there is usually an arrow at the top and at the bottom; clicking on these arrows will display the connections of the team in order of hierarchy, superiors or employees linked to this person, depending on whether the down or up arrow is selected. The inclusion of a picture in the profile is usually mandatory, depending on the company.

• • • •

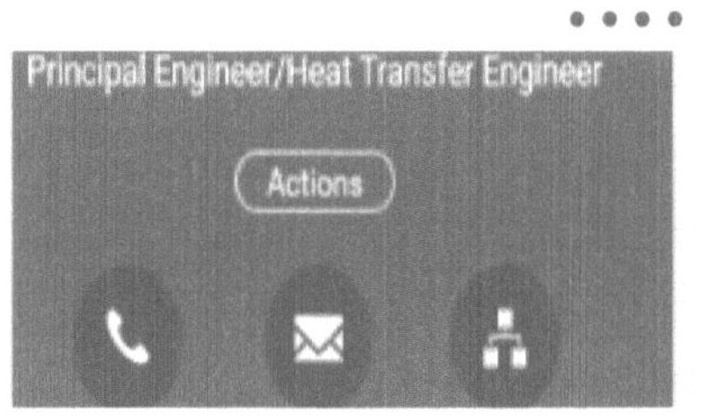

• • • •

To access the main information box, simply search for the employee's first surname or ID. There is always a printer icon at the top of the main box, which when clicked, displays a number of information sheets, usually in Excel, containing 100% of the data held for that person in the Workday database, which can be printed or saved, either in Excel or PDF format.

• • • •

Exemple: Employee transfer and position change.

Un employee has been promoted and will move into another office, in different city. HR must to update her contract including the news changes, salary, new office, new position, starting date and more. For this purpose, the company has several specific web pages where you can check the employee's data, the existing and the new assignment, as well as the new salary, hours, and so on.

By checking these sites, the HR team can easily update the data corresponding to the contract renewal. Alternatively, they can do this within Workday through the 'Integration' system and confirm with the managers or hiring manager, who will typically be the ones to manage the final acceptance of the new changes.

The whole process can be done almost entirely within Workday or Service Now, using some support software such as Skype Business to interact with managers without the need for annoying phone calls and to get the appropriate validations in a consistent way.

• • • •

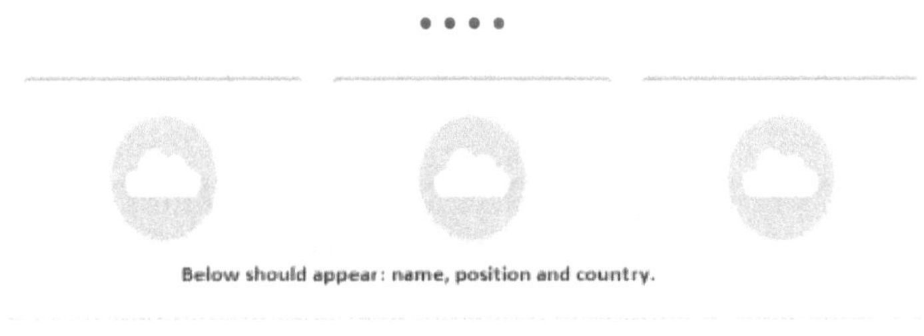

• • • •

Workday is used by many companies to provide direct access to their job vacancies. All you need to do is register on the access portal with an email address and password. You will immediately receive an up-to-date and detailed list of the company's vacancies. To apply, simply click on the job title and download the relevant documents quickly and easily.

The Employee Self-Service Portal is easy to access and use and covers all the basic needs of employees, from a simple click to enter their schedule, to viewing schedules, requesting time off, downloading personal documents, a diverse core of options to facilitate the employee/company relationship on an ongoing basis. Supervisors and managers have the same advanced features and access levels, depending on the company's qualifications.

Many of the functions are easy to perform, with a day icon in the drop-down calendar offering the various options immediately without any major hiccups. Other options, especially for new staff, often have the inconvenience of repeated 'errors' appearing on the screen, preventing tasks from being completed.

These are almost always basic handling issues, such as the inclusion of a space, or the incorrect entry of a required date or name. In these cases, the employee usually needs to contact the company's helpdesk (or a third party) to find a solution.

• • • •

Service now: an Integration Option with Workday.

• • • •

ServiceNow is a leading cloud-based platform that offers a wide range of services for enterprise IT service management (ITSM), as well as broader business operations management. ServiceNow is well-known for its ITSM capabilities, providing the option for organizations to manage and streamline IT service delivery, incident management, problem management, change management, and other IT-related processes, promoting efficiency and collaboration among IT teams.

The platform provides tools for automating various service processes, reducing manual tasks, and improving service delivery speed and consistency, includes a service catalog feature that enables organizations to create and manage a catalog of services offered to employees and customers, then users request services from this catalog.

ServiceNow offers IT asset management capabilities, promoting the organizations track and manage their IT assets, including hardware, software, and licenses. The platform includes a robust workflow and orchestration engine which enhances the ability of organizations to design and automate complex business processes, not limited to IT but also applicable to various other departments.

In addition to ITSM, ServiceNow has expanded into customer service management (CSM), providing tools for organizations to manage customer support and service requests. Offers security operations capabilities for managing and responding to security incidents and vulnerabilities effectively.

ServiceNow operates on a single-tenant architecture, which means that each customer gets their own copy or copies of ServiceNow in the cloud. These copies are called ServiceNow instances.

Each instance can run multiple applications side-by-side, so a single instance could potentially host an ITSM, HR, CSM and custom apps all on the same base URL. This allows ServiceNow to act as a single system of record for multiple business applications, enriching each application by sharing data.

For example, the HR application could trigger an employee onboarding workflow, which in turn creates a series of requests in the ITSM application to set up the new employee's computer.

Occasionally, you may come across organisations with only two or more than three instances, and even other labels such as QA, Staging or Sandbox. Using multiple instances in this way allows developers to work in non-prod instances and encourages development to follow a standardised process. This ensures that changes to the instance (such as customising forms or adding new code) can be thoroughly tested before being promoted to the prod environment.

ServiceNow's HR service delivery module helps organizations streamline HR processes, including employee onboarding, HR case management, and HR document management. Provides integration capabilities to connect with other systems and tools, it permits for seamless data exchange and workflow automation.

The platform includes reporting and analytics features giving to organizations gain insights into their service performance and make data-driven decisions. ServiceNow offers mobile apps and a mobile-friendly interface.

ServiceNow is highly customizable, enabling organizations to tailor it to their specific needs and integrate it with other systems through APIs; is widely used across various industries and is known for its flexibility and scalability. It is often used to drive digital transformation initiatives and improve operational efficiency.

· · · ·

Using Slack and/or RingCentral to receive calls.

· · · ·

We can use Slack to make calls, including voice and video calls. Slack offers communication features that will give us a variety of options for connect with our team members and colleagues in various ways.

We might initiate voice or video calls with individual users or colleagues by opening a direct message (DM) with them and clicking on the phone or camera icon at the top of the chat window. This will start a one-on-one call.

In addition to one-on-one calls, we can also create group calls within a Slack channel or group message. Simply click the phone or camera icon in a channel or group chat to start a call with multiple participants.

Slack can integrate with third-party calling and conferencing apps, such as Zoom, Microsoft Teams, or Google Meet. If our organization uses these services, we can initiate calls from within Slack by integrating the respective app. Slack offers screen sharing during video calls, making it easy to collaborate and present information to colleagues.

Slack's mobile apps for iOS and Android also support voice and video calls, enabling us to make calls from our mobile device while on the go. Slack provides settings to configure the microphone, camera, and audio devices for calls. We can access these settings from the call interface.

In this specific case, this software will be the internal support of the workgroup, contacts with those working at home, and all kinds of input regarding contacts with workgroups in other cities. The back and forth dynamic is extended with the corresponding supervisors and managers.

We need a program to receive customer service calls. *Ring Central* will be the one. *RingCentral* offers a unified communications platform that combines voice, video, messaging, and team collaboration tools into a single, integrated solution. This unified approach aims to enhance productivity and streamline communication within organizations.

RingCentral provides voice over internet protocol (VoIP) services, enabling users to make and receive calls over the internet. It offers features like call forwarding, call routing, and voicemail.

RingCentral Video is a video conferencing and online meeting solution that allows users to host and join video meetings, webinars, and screen sharing sessions. It includes features like HD video, chat, and integration with other collaboration tools. RingCentral includes team messaging and collaboration features, allowing teams to chat, share files, and collaborate in real time. It also provides integrations with popular messaging apps.

The platform offers contact center solutions for customer support and engagement. These solutions include features for call routing, interactive voice response (IVR), and analytics to improve customer service.

RingCentral provides integration capabilities with a wide range of third-party applications and services, including CRM systems, productivity tools, and cloud storage platforms. RingCentral offers mobile apps for iOS and Android devices, enabling users to access communication and collaboration tools while on the go.

• • • •

Company domain > Sign in > username > next

• • • •

The platform includes analytics and reporting features to help organizations gain insights into their communication patterns and performance. RingCentral emphasizes security and compliance, offering features like encryption, access controls, and compliance with various data protection regulations.

With ring Central users can customize their communication settings and workflows to suit their specific needs. Customization options may include call routing rules, IVR configurations, and more.

RingCentral is a Voice over Internet Protocol service. At its most basic, VoIP is a protocol that allows users to make telephone calls over an internet connection rather than a traditional landline. The software does not require any physical support (telephone), a headset is sufficient to receive calls.

The interactive menu offers the necessary options for an agent, on-hold, call time verification and other functions necessary for the constant improvement of the service. The agent needs its own individual access password. The time of access of the agent will be used by HR and management staff to monitor the reference time of connection to the service and compliance with the working day.

It also delivers the needs for varied and accurate reporting of all evolving tasks business needs and useful features. RingCentral essentially acts as a comprehensive communications package, proposing a much more efficient, cost-effective and streamlined solution than consuming and paying for several separate services simultaneously.

RingCentral also offers extensive integration with productivity and industry-specific third-party platforms like Slack. Easy administration, Works on any device, AI-powered tools built in, Reliable and persistent voice.

Unifying all of the company's communications into a single system is a lot more convenient than dealing with a bunch of separate apps and services, and it could reduce the overhead in the long term if company is currently paying for stuff don't need or if disorganized communications are slowing down the workflow.

• • • •

Sales Force Ticketing.

• • • •

Let's take a basic ticket creation situation. We work in retail, there has been contact with a customer, either by phone, email, chat, internally, whatever, and we need to create a ticket. It is not the same to create a basic and very simple ticket as it is to create a ticket following all the options offered by the programme.

The number of templates is large and facilitates the elaboration and subsequent monitoring of the incident, both for the agent himself and for the necessary concretions of supervisors and managers.

• • • •

Basic ticket template:
Subject (Till/Device/Issue/Error).
Store name and store #.
Employee First Name/Title/Extension.
Description of the issue/error.
Last button or last action performed prior to error.
Device/application/program affected.
Serial #/tablet#/Mode/Brand/Register#
# of tills in store.
# of tills affected.
Store Access Hours.

Troubleshooting:
A - customer and L1 Actions + KB
R - Results (troubleshooting outcome).
R - L1 recommendation/next steps.

There are many variants, many data that we take, that will facilitate our individual work or that of the group in which we are, the contacts with third parties and that will give grouped in groups (several tickets) the possibility to managers and other managers of the company to make monitoring statistics or various reports and service improvement, while offering internally the possibility to delimit more clearly the individual progress of employees.

• • • •

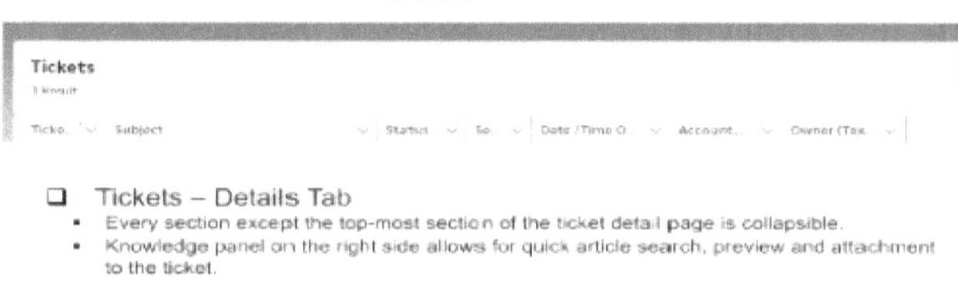

Working with Tills on the store (Ticket).

Subject Description: Till 11- not printing receipts- not error message.

Subject (Till/Device/Issue/Error): Till 11 is not printing receipts.
Employee First Name/Title/Extension: Julie- Store Manager.
Description of the issue/error: Receipt printing is not show up.
Last button or last action performed prior to error: payment with credit card.
Device/application/program affected: Receipt printer of Till 11. Serial#/Tablet#/Model/Brand/Register#: 123456748971.
Store Access Hours: M-Sa 9:30a-8p Closed Sundays.

· · · ·

New ticket > Request type > Incident

· · · ·

Troubleshooting: Customer called in to report that receipt printer for Till 11 is not printing receipts. Customer already tried reseating cables and restarting the till and it still won't print. Printer is on and lights are on.

Customer also mentioned that she has changed the printer paper and cleaned the printer. Asked her permission to reprofile till. Restarted the till but still unable to print. Receipt printer is still not printing despite troubleshooting listed above. We will need to replace the device. We must to escalate for technician actions on-site.

· · · ·

As supervisors/managers, we create diferent folders in order to include select tickets for our team. For example, 'tickets pending for this week', 'tickets by employees shift', any desired option will be created and then we will save the connected tickets in each folder, giving access to employees if desired for easier handling and concretisation.

New ticket > Customer information > name> contact email > Ticket description > Submit

• • • •

Making Collections.

We are now doing debt collection in the healthcare sector, the sale of medical equipment to hospitals, for a company called ZSZA. Our tasks are varied, from tracking the delivery of the equipment (for example, an ultrasound machine), issuing tax receipts, allocations in the event of contract changes, liaising with the credit department and, of course, following up on progress with the customer or requests for non-payment.

• • • •

INSTALLATION DEED

Equipment available for first patient examination: (Date)

Client Representative

| (Name) | (Position) |

| (Signature) | (Date) |

ZSZA representative

| (Name) | (Position) |

| (Signature) | (Date) |

Additional Order Information:

The equipment has been installed and is ready to perform the first patient examination, except for the following contractually agreed functionality.

All functionalities have been delivered.

Non-delivered products or services contractually agreed.

The Equipment Acceptance' Deed must be followed up and verified in its entirety, with a form similar to that of the Installation Deed, including all the signatures indicated.

The equipment covered by the contract, an ultrasound system, has been installed and ZSZA Healthcare (Electromedical Devices) certifies that it is in substantial conformity with the technical specifications offered. The installation process has been completed with the exception of the minor outstanding issues described below.

The customer's signature indicates that the equipment is ready for the first patient examination. ZSZA remains liable for any contractual agreements not yet delivered.

delivered.

Installation completed: The equipment covered by the contract has been installed at the customer's designated site and has been electronically and mechanically tested to operate in accordance with the technical specifications provided by ZSZA. The equipment is ready for the first patient test.

The customer acknowledges that the warranty period begins on 16 February 2015 and ends on 15 February 2016 (1 year).

• • • •

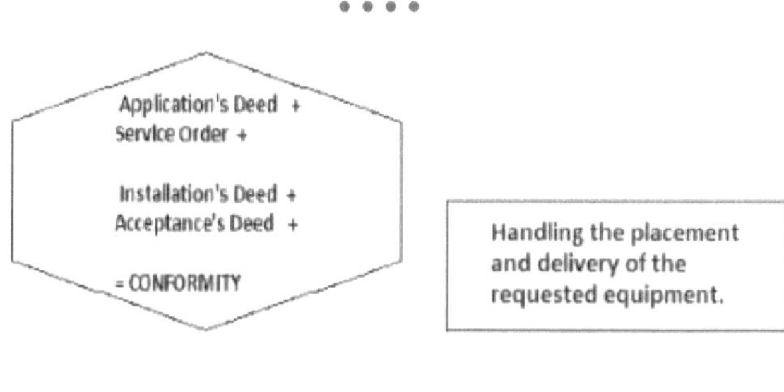

• • • •

As Projet Manager, our profile and responsabilities are: be the main interface between company and customer, make sure and enhance the customers' satisfaction, and feedback on the customer's concern positively, and coordinate the communication between company and customers closely. GRAFICO

Let's review now the responsibilities as Collections specialists:

Collections specialists are responsible for resolving overdue bills and collecting payments from the individuals or businesses responsible for the debt. They must locate those responsible for unpaid bills and set up acceptable terms of repayment to protect the financial assets of their employer.

Common responsibilities for a collections specialist will include: Identifying accounts with overdue payments and keeping records of the amount owed and the length of the delinquency. Locating debtors and contacting them via phone or mail to address their overdue payments and determine the reason for the outstanding debt.

<table>
<tr><td>

DETAiLS
Terminologies
- FBL5N
- FBO3
- XDO3
- Service Invoice
- Equipment Invoice
- Sending of Invoices
- Exporting from SAP using FBL5N
   Open Line Items

</td><td>

- Using the macro
- TABS (explained)
- Present accounts
- Sending of SOA during first week of the fiscal calendar
- Sending SOA depending of customers request
- Sending SOA after payment was done. follow up
- Calling customer if they received the invoices electronically and if invoices are correct
- Calling customer to collect past due invoices
- Calling customers to for proactive collections p2p amount, date of payment
- From Peter's account to Mary's account
- Emails received asking for receipts
- Analytics concept of the receipt/percent of prepayment calculation
- Analytics convertion

</td></tr>
</table>

Communicating with the sales department to maintain accurate and updated information on client accounts and payments. Contacting customers to inform on delinquency, encourage on-time payments and set up payment plans that can facilitate good credit.

Processing customer payments, account adjustments and customer refunds where appropriate. Reviewing records for accuracy and handling disputes to make sure that account information is entered and maintained appropriately.

Reconciliation of account. Update desktop procedure, in order to manage Latam countries and meetins/collections. Using the employer's call center software (SAP). Understanding debt collection laws and regulations. Negotiating with clients.

Negotiations often take place as collections specialists are working out payment plans with their clients and their debtors. These professionals must be able to negotiate successfully and come to agreements that benefit all parties.

Managing collections requires argbiem-solving when finding the best way to manage clients and debtors. Collections specialists should be comfortable investigating complex issues to better understand these matters.

As Projet Manager, our profile and responsabilities are: be the main interface between company and customer, make sure and enhance the customers' satisfaction, and feedback on the customer's concern positively, and coordinate the communication between company and customers closely.

We will follow the project site schedule, control the project risk, and improve the project profit. We will make sure the project KPI by excellent planning, supervising, and controlling.

We will be responsible for the factory acceptance test and manufacture supervisor from customers, Arrange the site service with after sales service department. We will be responsible for the project payment collection.

We will assist the financial department in evaluating the project risk, analyzing the cost, and controlling the cost. Living ZSZA core values of safety and integrity means taking responsibility for our actions while caring for our colleagues and the business.

Conclusion

Brain science constantly studies the brain structure and the underlying mechanism of emotions. In combination with the continuous simulation of the human brain by Artificial Intelligence, this article builds on the mechanism of emotional perception in the human brain and designs the classification of implicit reasoning attributes to mimic the brain structure related to emotion.

Implicit reasoning information is introduced through multi-task learning as auxiliary information to recognise AI-reasoning, enhancing the effect of speech emotion recognition and demonstrating the effectiveness of the network proposed in this work.

In the future, we will be able to learn from the human brain's cognitive emotion mechanism and add more attribute information. In the meantime, we can also adopt different approaches instead of multi-task learning to reason about AI information.

In this context, we have mentioned and reinforced several ideas, including the need to be very critical. "I mean, not everything AI says is true. Not at all. It has hallucinations. It makes mistakes. Sometimes it gives a wrong result, information that doesn't seem to exist. We need to know that there is an algorithm that prioritises some things over others and the search engine is not showing us that.

We need to be critical in order to determine the truth of the answers, and increasingly at younger and younger ages. A child today needs to think much more critically than they did 30 years ago, when life was simpler and they were not faced with a whirlwind of truths and lies as they are today. Correlating different options in a package that contains many 'lies' requires additional filters.

To distinguish right from wrong, young people (and ourselves) need to be re-educated to ensure that they are prepared for the digital environment they will encounter. This is the only way to ensure that they do not make mistakes with this technology. It will not be easy, but there is no other way. Bans in this area would only lead to more acceptance by young people, in a dimension of rejection of the one who bans. That would be disastrous.

Artificial Intelligence is welcome. But the question is, where does it take us as a social cluster?. What will be its uses in terms of social cohesion?. Is Artificial Intelligence going to create a new world, or is it going to transform this one, the one we have been in and the one we have now?.

We have also analysed, from our point of view, what are the advantages and disadvantages of artificial intelligence. Artificial neural networks and deep learning AI technologies are quickly evolving, primarily because AI can process large amounts of data much faster and make predictions more accurately than humanly possible.

While the huge volume of data created on a daily basis would bury a human researcher, AI applications using machine learning can take that data and quickly turn it into actionable information.

As of this writing, a primary disadvantage of AI is that it is expensive to process the large amounts of data AI programming requires. As AI techniques are incorporated into more products and services, organizations must also be attuned to AI's potential to create biased and discriminatory systems, intentionally or inadvertently.

Among the most important disadvantages we could point out, that requires deep technical expertise, it is expensive, limited supply of qualified workers to build AI tools, lack of ability to generalize from one task to another, eliminates human jobs, increasing unemployment rates, reflects the biases of its training data, at scale.

In terms of advantages, reduced time for data-heavy tasks, saves labor and increases productivity, delivers consistent results, can improve customer satisfaction through personalization and certainly AI-powered virtual agents are always available.

We hear a lot of talk that AI is going to change the labour market. What does this mean? There are many who agree in general that AI will improve the working environment, that it will destroy, or is already killing jobs, but that it will generate new options in a dynamic environment of constant job creation and employment support.

Theoretically, it sounds very promising, i.e. that it can provide new options and supposedly create new positions. If a carpet salesman asks us what benefits the use of AI can bring to him or her, what should I tell him or her? In reality, he or she wants to sell carpets, that his or her business works, that sales are good, that his or her business can grow.

Does AI serve as an orientation for all types of professions, or will it only be oriented to certain fields, that would be a serious open question for a new future text.

Moreover, because no one is explaining clearly where this situation is leading us, what kind of society is intended to create, because if there is going to be a succession of novelties, of new jobs, given that some professions are impacted by the use of technology leaving their function obsolete or meaningless for the youngest, what is the orientation as a society that this entails.

Somebody somewhere, individually or collectively, somebody, I mean, must be using and directing all this technological creation for premeditated purposes. It wouldn't hurt to know some of the real objectives of this planning.

It makes a lot of sense to favour young people, they are the future, but the reality is that they are not very convinced by the use of the technological environment, they use it in the same way as they use social networks by inertia, but they do not transmit the feeling of conviction of abundance, on the contrary, cases of psychological problems, new diseases and passivity, a lot of lethargy, appear. We need to change this dynamic.

On the other hand, mathematics, are renowned for its precision and ability to model complex phenomena. Mathematical modeling provides a systematic framework to understand, simulate, and predict real-world processes. This precision will be harnessed across diverse disciplines, including physics, biology, and engineering. However, its potential extends even further when combined with linguistic approaches.

The fusion of linguistic and mathematical approaches involves using mathematical tools to analyze linguistic data. Natural Language Processing (NLP), a field at the intersection of linguistics and computer science, exemplifies this synergy.

The interdisciplinary approach is not limited to a few fields but has the potential to revolutionize research in countless areas. As technology continues to advance, the collaboration between linguists, mathematicians, and researchers from various domains will only become more vital in addressing the multifaceted challenges of our rapidly evolving world.

We have also explored how the fusion of linguistic and mathematical approaches significantly enhance interdisciplinary research. By combining the precision and abstraction of mathematics with the richness and complexity of language, researchers gain deeper insights and develop innovative solutions to a wide range of interdisciplinary challenges.

The connotations derived from how AI does or does not affect creativity also have their own little space within the narrative. There have been a few examples who, from their own calmness of reasoning, have reiterated the version of the hidden imaginary that seeks to convey a voice of madness as well as congeniality.

The main negative changes come down to a simple but now quite difficult question: How can we see, and fully understand the implications of, the algorithms programmed into everyday actions and decisions?.

The rub is this: Whose intelligence is it, anyway?. Our systems do not have, and we need to build in, should be the ability to not only create technological solutions but also see and explore their consequences before we build business models, companies and markets on their strengths, and especially on their limitations.

The overall impact of ubiquitous algorithms is presently incalculable because the presence of algorithms in everyday processes and transactions is now so great, and is mostly hidden from public view. All of our extended thinking systems (algorithms fuel the software and connectivity that create extended thinking systems) demand more thinking – not less – and a more global perspective than we have previously managed.

The expanding collection and analysis of data and the resulting application of this information can cure diseases, decrease poverty, bring timely solutions to people and places where need is greatest, and dispel millennia of prejudice, ill-founded conclusions, inhumane practice and ignorance of all kinds.

Our algorithms are now redefining what we think, how we think and what we know. We need to ask them to think about their thinking – to look out for pitfalls and inherent biases before those are baked in and harder to remove.

To create oversight that would assess the impact of algorithms, first we need to see and understand them in the context for which they were developed. That, by itself, is a tall order that requires impartial experts backtracking through the technology development process to find the models and formulae that originated the algorithms. Then, keeping all that learning at hand, the experts need to soberly assess the benefits and deficits or risks the algorithms create. Who is prepared to do this?.

Personal assessments are the embers of a boldness that is nourished by experience and evolution within the group that regularly gives its opinion on the contributions of AI.

Thus, we have established scales for changes in work, software evolutionary patterns, differences between company departments, customer service programmes, customer contact actions, communication facilities with management, among others, always in the dynamics of interest in getting to know how AI can think, how it can reason in its domains and meet the emotions of its interlocutors.

As we have seen, there are many contributions of artificial intelligence in many areas, but we must never forget that its use may serve for good or bad. The real challenge in the face of artificial intelligence is to educate the critical thinking of future generations so that they can adequately make suitable usage of a tool that is of maximum utility, without a doubt, that will make the world simpler in many aspects and that will bring us solutions that we could not even imagine.

We must lose our fear of AI, it is a tool that we people have invented and that will make our lives easier. It will give us time to do more things because it will take care of those tedious tasks and will carry them out with great accuracy and speed by handling all the data that has been administered to it very well. So I think this concept of AI as a co-pilot, helping us with tasks, with evolving, is really positive.

Today, AI is increasingly present in science and society and, if the trend continues, it will play a central role in tomorrow's education and jobs. It unavoidably interacts with other fields of science, and in this document we have examined the ways in which these interactions can lead to mutually synergistic outcomes.

We focused our observations on the mutual benefits that can be reaped from these interactions and emphasise the significant role of interdisciplinarity in this process. AI systems have complex lifecycles, including data acquisition, training, testing and deployment, which eventually requires an interdisciplinary approach to auditing and assessing the quality and security of these AI products or services.

Furthermore we have targeted on how AI practitioners can prevent biases through transparency, explainability, and how robustness, security and data privacy can and should be ensured.

In bottom line, we have insisted on a compendium of doubts that absorb the daily life of those who want to follow the path of the inescapable. There is no turning back, AI has been invading the different evolutionary aspects of society and will continue to do so more and more in the foreseeable future. The question is more about how to adapt to this changing environment, rather than getting carried away by doubts. after all, a changing and aggressive society needs diversified and powerful tools.

References

Acks, A. *The Bubble of Confirmation Bias: Critical Thinking about Digital Media.* Enslow Publishing. New York, 2018.

Betz, F.. *Strategic thinking: A Comprehensive guide.* Emerald Group Publishing, UK. 2016.

Bhoopchand, A., Brownfield, B., Collister, A. et al. *Learning few-shot imitation as cultural transmission.* Nat Commun 14, 7536, 2023. https://doi.org/10.1038/s41467-023-42875-2

Corcoran, J., *Aristotle's Prior analytics and Boole's Laws of Thought.* History and Philosophy of Logic, 24(4), 261–288, 2003. https://doi.org/10.1080/01445340310001604707

Digital Regulation Platform, 11.09.2023. *Transformative technologies (AI) challenges and principles of regulation.* https://digitalregulation.org/3004297-2/

Smith K. Khare. *Emotion recognition and AI: A systematic review.* Volume 102, February 2024. https://www.sciencedirect.com/science/article/pii/S1566253523003354

Davis, E., and Marcus G. *Commonsense reasoning and commonsense knowledge in artificial intelligence.* Communications of the ACM, 58(9):92–103, 2015.

Greiner, Ray. and Metes, George. *Going Virtual.* Upper Saddle River, Prentice-Hall, 1995.

Halton, Clay. *Predictive Analytics: Definition, Model Types, and Uses.* January 30, 2023. https://www.investopedia.com/terms/p/predictive-analytics.asp

Handy, Charles B. *The Age of Paradox.* Harvard Business School Press, 1994.

Hendrycks, Dan., Burns, Collin. UC Berkeley. *Measuring Mathematical Problem Solving With the MATH Dataset, 2017.* https://arxiv.org/pdf/2103.03874.pdf

Jinsong, Li. *Emotion Recognition Using Different Sensors, Emotion Models, Methods and Datasets: A Comprehensive Review.* https://www.mdpi.com/1424-8220/23/5/2455

Oluwatobi Ayodeji Akanbi, Elahe Fazeldehkordi, in *A Machine-Learning Approach to Phishing Detection and Defense: k-Nearest Neighbors Algorithm.* Elsevier Inc. 2005. https://www.sciencedirect.com/topics/computer-science/k-nearest-neighbors-algorithm

Peters, Tom. *Thriving on Chaos.* New York. Wings, 1995.

Pólya. G. *How to Solve It.* Princeton University Press, 1945.

Rumelt, R. *Good Strategy/Bad Strategy: Why It Matters.* London. Profile Books, 2011.

Szegedy C., *A promising path towards autoformalization and general AI.* In CICM, 2020.

Urwin, Richard. *Artificial Intelligence,* Arcturus Publishing Ltd., 2016.

World Bank Group. *Credit Scoring Approaches Guidelines,* 2009. https://thedocs.worldbank.org/en/doc/935891585869698451-0130022020/original/CREDITSCORINGAPPROACHESGUIDELINESFINALWEB.pdf

Yejin Choi. *The Curious Case of Commonsense Intelligence.* Published under a CC BY-NC 4.0 license, 2022. https://www.amacad.org/publication/curious-case-commonsense-intelligence

About the Author

Jorge Argibay holds a Master's degree in Comparative Literature from Autonoma University of Madrid, where he won the research award. This degree was combining with stays at the French University Paris-Diderot (Paris 7). He is a breath of contrasting knowledge in the field of interpretation, literary studies and the academic environment, with a touch of gentle lethargy.

He has extensive international experience and has immersed himself in the geography of countries as diverse as Mexico, Colombia, France, United Kingdom, China and the Philippines, in a constant quest to study other languages and cultural interactions. He has worked as an interpreter, teacher and researcher. He has applied his knowledge in the business world, by supporting multilingual teams in their task of recruiting new talent. His mind has been able to adapt to his obsession for travel itineraries, combining his admiration for other cultures, mixing it all in the same cocktail of his own destiny.